Irish Women:
Image and
Achievement

Mother and Child, stained glass panel by Evie Hone, Kildare County Library (Courtesy Arts Council of Ireland)

Irish Women: Image and Achievement

Women in Irish culture from earliest times

Edited by Eiléan Ní Chuilleanáin

ARLEN
HOUSE
The Women's Press

British Library Cataloguing in Publication Data
Irish Women: Image and Achievement.
1. Women — Ireland — Social conditions
1. Ní Chuilleanáin, Eiléan
305.4'2'09415   HQ1600.3

ISBN 0—905223—61—6
ISBN 0—905223—66—7 Pbk

Design and layout by Ditty Kummer

Typesetting by Gifford & Craven

Printing by O'Brien Promotions

Cover Photographs
Nóirín Ní Riain, (RTE)
Eiléan Ní Chuilleanáin, (Fergus Bourke)

This book is published with the assistance of the Arts Council
(An Chomhairle Ealaíon)

First published 1985 by Arlen House, 69 Jones Road, Dublin 3,
Ireland.

CONTENTS

LIST OF ILLUSTRATIONS

Preface and Acknowledgements

This book originated in a series of lectures on 'The Irish Woman' delivered as part of a tour known as the 'Irish Fortnight' in various American cities in March and April 1979. The tour was organised by the Irish-American Cultural Institute, whose President, Professor Eoin McKiernan, has long been promoting original work in the field of Irish culture. With the exception of the two by Nuala O'Faolain and Yvonne Scannell, all the present essays are based on lectures given on that tour. As well as the authors represented here, Anne Clune and Cliona McMahon also delivered lectures, and there were performances by Micheál Ó Suilleabháin (with Nóirín Ní Riain) and May Cluskey.

After we had returned to Ireland, Dr Margaret MacCurtain and I discussed the possibility of editing the lectures to form a book that would in some sense be a sequel to *Women in Irish Society* (Arlen House 1978) edited by Margaret MacCurtain and Donncha Ó Corráin. That was mainly historical in emphasis, and the idea was that this book would in the first place supplement it and in the area of legal change bring it up to date, and in the second place extend the discussion of women's place in Irish society to include women's artistic achievements and the place women have occupied in the development of the Irish imagination, as the emphasis in the lecture series had been on mythology, folklore and the arts. All of the essays have been re-written and two, by Nuala O'Faolain and Yvonne Scannell, are entirely new. My thanks are due to all the contributors for the patience, good humour and industry which they brought to this task. I should like to thank James Daly in particular for his kindness in making the late Miriam Daly's work available to me. Thanks are also due to Eileen Black, Pearse Hutchinson, J.J. Lee, Proinsias MacCana, Patrick MacEntee, Vivien Mercier and Christopher Woods, for help, advice and criticism.

Eiléan Ní Chuilleanáin
DUBLIN 1985

Women in Doorway, etching by Estella F. Solomons (Arts Council of Ireland)

Introduction

Eiléan Ní Chuilleanáin

The word 'image' in the title of this book refers in the first place to a social and historical image of women, the one devised by the folk-imagination, evidenced in the work of the anonymous stone-carver, inspiring the law-giver and the revolutionary. In the second place it refers to images of the world devised by women themselves, as they liberate themselves, through achievement in their work, and through their vision and insight as artists, from servitude to an image that has been imposed from without. The image created by woman herself may supersede the one presented to her by history and society, but she remains a member of society, an inter-preter of history, and thus can never ultimately separate herself from a historical image of the feminine.

These two meanings of 'image' — ideas *about* women, and ideas held things made *by* women — led to the sorting of the essays into two groups. The first group includes essays on early Irish history, mythology and archaeology, on the position of women in Irish society from Celtic origins to the foundation of the Free State in 1922, and on the legal changes (and the resistance to change) which have brought about a partial revolution in Irish women's position today. The second group repeats this pattern of historical development from unknown origins in folk-culture, but this time in the field of the arts: folk-music, craft-work, Gaelic poetry and the work of modern painters, sculptors and writers.

I have given these groups the names 'image' and 'achievement', but of course the two are complementary: the image of woman as a dependant, for example, has been important in the framing of laws which limited the area of what a woman could achieve, and the achievement of the woman artist involves the creation of images. These groupings, adopted for con-venience. should not obscure certain oppositions within them. In the group labelled 'image' there is a contrast between such flamboyant female figures as the Sheela-na-gig, the banshee and the powerful Celtic Christian saints, and the abstractions on which laws, working conditions and historical movements are fed. Neither the historian's statistics nor the potent myths are human beings. The human being must find herself between the two and for much of history the reality of her life is simply lost to us.

Images of Women: Myth and Reality

The benign figure of St Brigid, the horrific badhb and the obscene Sheela-na-gig derive their force from a sense of primal drama in which it is impossible, as with the banshee of more recent folklore, to separate the being from her sex or from her function and setting. Both the image of woman envisaged in the Irish constitution as housebound wife and mother and the revolutionary woman in the mould of Countess Markiewicz owe something to the myth-making faculty. Both figures appear in a context in which the separation of a woman from her role, her sexual function, her background and her country itself can be discussed. Irish emigrant women briefly mentioned by Margaret MacCurtain and Miriam Daly, and Irish women deprived of their social position by the desertion and emigration of their husbands, whom Yvonne Scannell treats, represent the extreme of the divorce between the childlike acceptance of myths that speak to the collective unconscious and the hard facts of some lives, of many women's lives in Irish history and many women's lives in Ireland today.

So the study of the Irish woman's image through history is also the study of the gap, most easily appreciated for the last couple of centuries, between that image and what many Irish women have actually experienced. And, coming from an awareness of the gap, it is also the history of the demand that Irish women be treated as human beings, that the freedom which many in fact exercised — if only by entering a convent or taking the boat to America or Australia — be recognised and institutionalised as part of the permanent structure of the society they lived in.

We study the history of woman by studying feminine images because, while much of orthodox history has simply left women out, the human imagination has never been able to do so. Feared, reverenced or sentimentally diminished, the feminine image has always been present. In learning about it, women may reach that sense of their own past which has always been one of the aims of history. 'To be ignorant about what happened before one was born is to remain a child forever' is especially true for women, since the version of the past offered by old-fashioned history excluded them so firmly. Out of myths and legends, out of the occasional biographical fragment of an outstanding individual, the history of women emerges, not as a causally connected series of events but as a drama of human forces which gradually formalises to articulate a debate about women's nature, capabilities and position in the world.

The essays in this book, by scrutinising separate though occasionally overlapping fields of activity, bring into relief various aspects of women's situation and capabilities. It is beyond the scope of an introduction to synthesise all the details of these various expert analyses; and I have no desire to blur by paraphrase what the writers have to say, or to interpret them into an unreal consensus. But I do want to suggest some of the relationships that exist between the specialised areas under consideration, and to sketch briefly the relevance of some other areas. One of these is the degree of outside influence on the Irish view of life; another is the question of the image of women presented by Irish male writers. These conflicting influences, these rival versions of what it means to be a woman, are worth considering because of the psychological importance of images, and not merely to students of psychology or sociology, but to everybody.

Human beings make use of images as examplars to learn about life, to achieve maturity and to launch themselves towards the objects of their life's struggle. They identify and they are intimidated or they are inspired. Sexual identity in particular and the outlook on life, life considered as a series of possibilities, that accompanies sexual identification seem to be sharply conditioned by the available patterns of behaviour seen as inextricably connected with one or other sex. Not only the choices young people make, which deeply affect the later course of their lives, but the level of achievement that is possible to them in the directions they have chosen appear to be closely connected with the image they have formed of themselves. And this applies not only to vocational choice but to all the enterprises of life.

If there were a fuller history of women, it might not affect the kind of choice that we call instinctive. History may enter the individual's consciousness too late to influence the underlying patterns of personality in their first growth. Even school readers, even fairy stories, may not come close enough to the beginning of the child's view of the world, to do that. But if the history of women's fate and women's actions cannot create new people it can make available a wider variety of exemplars, able to instruct or to inspire as well as to equip with information.

The Irish Experience and Outside Influences

The Irish woman may be helped, by contemplating history, towards a maturity impossible without some sense of the past. But society too faces a problem: that of evolving an image of women and their rights, balancing those of men, which will be as truthful and as helpful as possible, and of embodying this vision in political, legal and social action. This action has to be carried out in Irish conditions and thus the nature of those conditions as they affect women has to be established. Questions arise: that of defining what is peculiar to Irish women's experience, and what outside influences have affected that experience.

In this book Helen Wood and Patricia Lysaght describe patterns of thought and imagery reaching back to Celtic prehistory and expressing themselves in ways that are unique to Ireland. But, as Margaret MacCurtain shows, Ireland, a country which has been invaded and colonised physically and politically, has also suffered a colonisation of minds and attitudes: the relatively free and powerful position enjoyed by women in Gaelic society was replaced by their relegation to domesticity and powerlessness under English common law. Outside influences have also contributed to women's emancipation, however: the French and American revolutions gave an impetus not only to Republican sentiment but also to the sense that the rights of man should include the rights of women. And in very recent years, as Yvonne Scannell shows, Ireland's membership of the European Community has forced a progressive legal emancipation of women on an unwilling male-dominated Irish legislature.

An important step in the liberation of Irish women has been the recognition that the laws of nature, of biology, economics and political power function in Ireland as they do elsewhere, and as elsewhere have been made to function to women's disadvantage. 'Irish solutions to Irish problems' — a catch-phrase coined by a government minister faced with the problem of devising a law on birth-control that would not alienate the Catholic Church — mean in the realm of women's experience a refusal to see that instead of the familiar stereotype of the Irish wife and mother there has risen to confront the legislator the universal figure of woman as a full member of the human race. And yet to scrutinise the predicament of women in the particular Irish context may save women from the sense of being doubly colonised, from the sense that all power to become fully conscious of her situation is earned at the cost of a blurring of the exact outlines of the situation by the adoption of a masculine or a priestly or a metropolitan perspective.

Dr MacCurtain refers to the usual opinion which connects the 'illiberal legislation and stifling provincialism' of the new Ireland of the twenties and thirties with the 'value system of a traditional-minded, rural orienstated society', and goes on to point out the importance of this state of affairs for the 'virtual exclusion of women from public life'. The laws of the Irish Free State, however, the philosophy of the 1937 constitution, the legislation, policies and social welfare provisions of the governments of the forties and fifties were not simply home-grown. The established morality had been deeply coloured by foreign influences.

Historians agree on the noticeable difference between Irish Catholic piety in the eighteenth and nineteenth centuries, and commentators in the twentieth century have remarked the existence of a special kind of Irish Catholic puritanism. The nineteenth century saw the introduction into Ireland by Italian missionary priests of Italian forms of religious organisation and observance and of the still ubiquitous Italian style of religious art, whose sexless, agonised depictions have certainly affected the imaginations of many generations of Irish children. In the same period, the Evangelical movement in the Church of England also mounted a missionary offensive in Ireland. A concern with temperance and a suspicion of all forms of pleasure or entertainment marked this movement, which also seems to have left its mark on Irish society in the late nineteenth century. The clash between these two missionary movements reinforced sectarian attitudes throughout the country.

In the early twentieth century Ireland was not, of course, the only traditionally minded society in the West. The degree of sympathy in Ireland with the Francoist side in the Spanish Civil War, represented as a crusade against godlessness and immorality, was considerable, notwithstanding the strong feeling among Republicans of support for the Spanish government. In the forties and fifties Ireland was exposed as never before to American ideas, after the isolation of the war years during which foreign developments seemed particularly irrelevant. It was a time of high emigration, but one when emigrants could afford to keep in touch with the home country. Ireland's emerging foreign policy was closely bound to America's and the absence of any language barrier meant that American books and especially films had an immediate impact. This Americanisation was often denounced from pulpits as immoral, but the Hollywood cinema of the time was subjected to deeply conservative trends in American society and the kind of film likely to be passed by the Irish censor and approved by clerical watchdogs as harmless entertainment presented a view of women that stressed domesticity and dependence, with marriage as the only possible happy ending.

The nature of American influence on the Irish conservative mind was more complex than the importation of screen images. American society in the aftermath of the Second World War witnessed a clash between conservative ideologies and the actual extreme openness and mobility of the society. The Catholic Church, powerful, articulate and accepted as never before in the United States was, from the point of view of Irish-Americans and of the Irish at home, extremely important.

Betty Friedan's *The Feminine Mystique*, which documents the rise in this period of commercial, journalistic and political propaganda about women's behaviour, interests and limitations, ignores religious attitudes except for one perceptive comment on 'Suggested Outline for Married Couples' from the Family Life Bureau of the Catholic Archdiocese of New York: 'Even the traditional resistance of religious orthodoxy is marked today with the manipulative techniques of psychotherapy.' Her point was that the attitude to women which stressed the family as first priority and work as merely selfish distraction, the romanticism of monogamy and the sufficiency of home to absorb all women's interest and energies, was not broadcast only as crude advertising propaganda or as entertainment, but was also articulated as psychological and sociological theory and thus presented to students and to the public interested in popular science as authoritative. She quotes the anthropologist Margaret Mead about the end result: 'Woman has gone back, each to her separate cave, waiting anxiously for her mate and children to return, guarding her mate jealously against other women, almost totally unaware of any life outside her door.'

And it was not only in America that conservative ideas were presented in the guise of modern science. The undergraduate textbooks in sociology and psychology which were in use in Irish universities and colleges in the fifties and sixties belonged to the same movement, as did the watered-down versions presented in schools and popular magazines under Church auspices. Censorship kept out of students' hands any book which discussed contraception; as textbooks in these subjects not written from a Catholic point of view were likely to do. In practice this tended to mean that British books were kept out and American Catholic ones admitted.

The contemporary women's movement began as a reaction against the stereotyped image of women so powerfully articulated by media and textbooks that led to the 'cave-woman' impasse. In Ireland the unprecedented prosperity of the sixties had made women, as long as they remained within the confines of the domestic world, actually capable of seeing themselves in the mould of the Western housewife, whose freedom consists in the lightening of the work of housekeeping and the buoyancy of her husband's pay-packet, canonised by society as wife, mother and consumer. Her troubles started if she tried to cross the barrier surrounding her domestic existence. She was at once confronted with problems that had nothing to do with the international advertisers' stereotype.

The Image of Women in the New Republic

The rhetoric of Irish Republicanism from which the state took its origin had stressed national unity embracing divergent traditions. Thus, it appeared to open the way to rejecting the dominance of one Christian Church and, by its stress on common humanity and the rights of man, to admit the rights of woman also. In so far as women have been affected by this ideology they are shown assuming identical responsibility with men's during periods of war, their rank, their actions described in the same language. The history of the Southern Irish state has not shown this equality of function surviving in peacetime. The view of woman expressed in the 1937 constitution, declaring that 'by her life within the home, woman gives the State a support without which the common good cannot be achieved', assigns to her a special sphere and assumes that all women, by reason of their sex, can be included in this image of the domesticated wife and mother. Not all Irish women married, however. For the century after 1860 single women formed a very high proportion of the population, as Dr MacCurtain points out, and of those who did marry, not all were satisfied with their lot, virtually excluded from the working population, at the mercy of their own fertility and hemmed in by the impossibility of escaping from unsatisfactory marriages. If we consider the images of women reflected in the society of the mid-century we can see how images may be used not always to unite but occasionally to divide and discriminate and to make genuine free choice impossible.

The Irish state's laws and social provisions up to 1970 remained repressive of liberty in the two areas of sex and work. The outlawing of contraception, the fact that women at work accepted lower wages and, if married, were taxed at a higher rate than men, had the result that in both areas women paid a higher price for less. A choice was offered by the state to women in its employment between work and marriage. It was a false choice, dividing economic autonomy from sexuality and commitment in personal life, but it made it easy to play off groups of women against each other, married against single and older against younger, since the marriage bar ensured that the majority of working women were young. As well as creating divisions between women, the marriage bar deprived the female image of the important elements of authority and maturity. It worked to the advantage of employers to have a large group in the labour force who could be expected to be docile, cheap (having in theory no dependants) and unlikely to organise because they expected not to stay at work long. The older woman at work, especially if she had achieved a degree of authority, was the object of some hostility from both men and younger women.

Another divisive image appeared when married women began their successful campaign for a change in the income tax laws. The minister for finance at the time dismissed the campaign as one of the 'well-heeled', sug̶ ̶ṣting that married women should be content to share their husbands' incomes. He was attempting on the one hand to drive a wedge between working and non-working married women and on the other to divide married and single women, assuming that the single would resent competition in the labour market from the married.

While in the forties and fifties Irish women married comparatively late and often did not marry at all, the proportion of married women in the population has risen sharply since the sixties. This has perhaps given rise to the appearance of greater progress by women than has in fact occurred. Concessions have been won in the areas of contraception, equal pay and equality of taxation, but they have been largely won by an appeal to the Irish constitution's declared aim of supporting the institution of marriage and the integrity of the family and thus represent a vindication of the rights of married people, rather than of women as persons with individual rights. The rights of the single woman, to contraception for instance, have made less progress.

The circumscribed freedom of the celibate woman worker, a freedom carefully planned not to threaten the interests of the prevailing system, can be contrasted with the vocation to religious celibacy. By contrast with the affirmation of the individual's sense of commitment, the deliberateness of the choice and the often outstanding work for the community that can follow the choice, the permission given to the working woman to fill a vacant space in the system is exposed as no choice at all. It merely continues what has always been the destiny of single women, servitude to a larger unit, whether one's own family, an employing family or firm, or the state.

If women in Ireland are to evolve a truthful image of themselves, one characteristic of such an image will be that, being created by women themselves and not assembled out of the catch-phrases of legislators and the obsessions of influential men who fear woman, it will unite women rather than dividing them. Where is one to look for the material for such an image? Firstly, in the creative potential which women have revealed in many areas but which can be readily studied in their achievements in the arts.

To wish to see one's experience reflected in the mirror of art is not narcissism but the desire for authentication and for a sense of objectivity. To feel and never find that feeling expressed by another is to experience not only isolation but unreality. To discover an expression of one's un-uttered thoughts, however remote in place or time, is a unique sensation of making contact with a solid world. Looking at women's performance in the arts we search, on the one hand, for authentic expression of what women have felt and thought, and at the same time we pay tribute to their achievement in taking us beyond what any ordinary person has managed to articulate.

Room was made for women as practitioners of the arts at an earlier stage in history than in other areas of non-manual activity. There has been the opportunity to develop maturity and to evolve techniques which suited them rather than borrowing from the male practitioner. The expectations of the audience too have matured. As well as reaching towards an excellence which she not only feels but can see lies within the scope of her sex, a woman artist may also aspire towards creating an image of herself and her sex from a femine point of view, and by a logical progression she arrives at an outlook on the whole of human experience which, by that originality of perspective, is able to explore what has been missed by the male vision.

Image of Women in Irish Literature

A subject that might well have been included among the present studies is just the Irish version of that male vision, and its relationship to the myths and stereotypes which have emerged into clarity from the examin-ation in the earlier half of the book. It is often a relationship of contrast. The single-minded, energetic women of Shaw's plays are part of the European revolt against the stereotype of the dependent, clinging female, though they tend also to endorse another stereotype: that of woman en-slaved by biology. Again, there is an evident contrast between the versions of femaleness offered by mythology, religion and folklore (Maeve, Sheela-na-gig, the Blessed Virgin, the banshee) and some twentieth-century literary heroines such as Molly Bloom, Patrick Pearse's *Mise Éire*, John McGahern's dying Elizabeth in *The Barracks* or the pro-tagonist of Brian Moore's *The Lonely Passion of Judith Hearne*. One group is charged with power, even the banshee. The other is distinguished by inertia, abandonment and isolation — even Mrs Bloom is never shown out of bed, however comfortable she may find it.

There is more than one reason why this should be so. Myth as such is incapable of falsification or prevarication. It cannot lie because it cannot stray beyond its own strictly limited truth. The marvellous, paradoxical or distorting effects which are special to myth when it enters literature may achieve otherwise impossible feats of communication. Molly Bloom's stored energy, her acquiescence that is not passivity, is felt by the reader not by virtue of any action, but at least partly because of the strength of the allusion to mythological associations between earth and motherhood.

Molly Bloom is a memorable articulation of the instinctive, receptive side of humanity, O'Casey's Juno of courage in the face of exhausting demands, Synge's Maurya of human dignity in the face of deprivation. That all three should be mothers of dead sons and living daughters is perhaps less important than the way none of them remains merely submerged in femininity, though the predicament of each is so inescapably connected with her femaleness. Each plays a part in an individually shaped work of art that shows, at least in the case of Joyce and Synge, originality of form and language as well as an original outlook on life.

As Nuala O'Faolain points out, the major male Irish writers have made considerable use of stereotypes in their presentation of female figures. The typical male classifications of women as virgin, mother and whore is, in the case of great writers, capable of being tragically or wittily handled — with conscious mythological reference as in Joyce or Yeats or to satiric purpose in the novels of Flann O'Brien and the novel-and-a-half of Patrick Kavanagh. The more direct, realistic presentation of the daily martyrdom of mothers and spinsters is often attempted in the Irish novel though less often producing a memorable work.

Artistic Achievement: Prestige and Value

The main emphasis of the essays in the second part of the book is, however, on what women artists have achieved in a wider sense than mere preoccupation with a female image. The historical circumstances, the lives and difficulties and the limitations of female artists have made differences in each case. As well as the special circumstances of the lace-maker or the folksinger, we have the individual talents and the often unconventional lives of artists. A look at these should restore a balance after much discussion of the typical and the average.

We may look at achievement in the arts as it is contained within the limits of traditional society. Folk-song and craft-work, anonymous as they are to us, carry prestige for the performer and the maker in her own circle. Or we may look at it as it is generally regarded in the modern world, where the artist is emancipated from dependence on a narrow circle and the work of art, too, can be contemplated in isolation from the society in which it originated.

It is pertinent to ask, if we are examining Ireland's treatment of women, including the women who have done work in the field of the arts, how that work has been valued. The anomalies discussed in the essays on history and law, in relation to pay and taxation, led to an undervaluing of female performance in the labour world. Activities whose value is regarded as intrinsic, not fixed by the market, include the arts; and the arts are thus likely to attract women escaping from a world in which what they do is devalued because it is they who do it.

But art is also the accompaniment of life lived under whatever social conditions, the measure and record of ordinary time. Nóirín Ní Riain discusses in her essay the fact that working women sing to pass the time — a trivial enough motive, one might think. The time might be paid for as the lace-makers' was at a niggardly rate. Miriam Daly recalls the efforts of Belfast employers to stop girls in linen factories from singing at their work, which led to a strike and ultimately to the girls' triumphant return to work, 'busy making up a song to sing as they go back', in James Connolly's words.

The emotional intensity of the female folk-song and the hostility of the factory bosses to women singing, suggest the importance of the arts not only as an expression of the talents of the exceptional and often extremely lucky individual, but as symbolising the resistance of humanity to being dehumanised, especially by inhuman conceptions of work.

Mary Coleman's study of the history of Irish lace reminds us of the whole stitched labyrinth of decorative, laborious, inventive work in which women specialised as pastime as well as for wages. Paula McCarthy's essay on women artists points out that the precursors of the modern painters and sculptors include craftswomen as well as young ladies who went to schools of art and travelled in Europe, and that women in the visual arts have been important as organisers and promoters, especially of communication between different generations of artists. The work of the lace-maker, the stained-glass artist or the novelist may emancipate the individual worker economically or spiritually, but it is not performed in isolation.

As a corollary to this social dimension of art, we must consider the relationship between the literary artist and her mass audience. Nuala O'Faolain examines this theme in the final essay in the book, arguing that there is a significant failure to produce an important feminist writer in modern Ireland. Her essay challenges not only the Irish tendency to set parochial standards in literature but the very dimensions of a study like this book. It is a challenge which relates to many of the considerations I have raised in this introduction and one well worth considering. But it too raises the question of the value of a woman's work; this time it is computed, not only by sales on a mass market, but by its power to reach the readers who, in twentieth-century conditions, can only be found by such a market.

I draw attention to this question of value because it enables me to make one final point about the double structure of this book. It is in the area of work that many of the most acute problems concerning women's position in society have arisen, whether in connection with admission to trades and professions, payment and taxation, or in the area of the home, with its alternatives of unpaid, burdensome housework or unwanted leisure filled with uncommercial activity, including craft-work. And it is in the context of women's experience that we can see most clearly the contradictions inherent in the way society regards work and its value.

The basic opposition is that between what a person is and what that person does. We claim to value what a person does. In practice it turns out to be impossible to do so without also considering what that person is. We must look at the image of the human being before we can begin to see the work with any clarity.

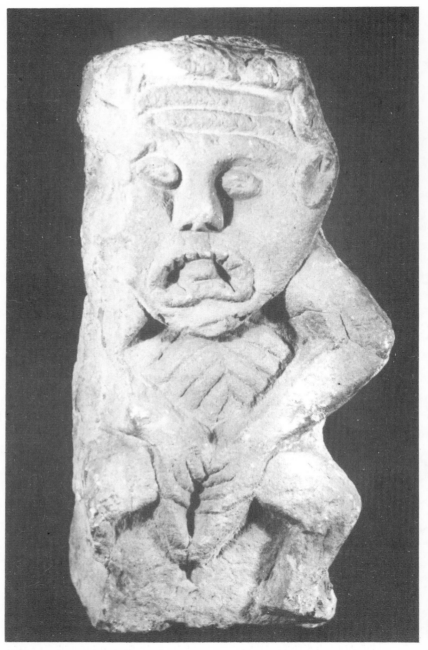

Sheela na gig, old church, Cavan (photograph, National Museum of Ireland)

Women in Myths & Early Depictions

Helen Lanigan Wood

Most of our information about women in prehistoric Ireland comes not from archaeology but from Irish mythology. From this source we can only surmise about the role of women in so for as it is reflected in that of legendary heroines and female deities who appear in early Irish literature. Mythology embraces a period in prehistory in which goddesses were worshipped as well as gods. These goddesses have many names and many characteristics, but basically their function is that of divine mother, concerned with fertility, with the protection of flocks and herds and with the security of the land and its people. A tri-functional female deity, Ériu, Fódla and Banbha, can be identified as the eponymous goddess of the whole land of Ireland. Another source of information, the study of Irish topographical names,[1] supports the evidence from mythology[2] in associating goddesses with natural features like hills, rivers, lakes and wells.

War Goddesses

While there is a certain amount of overlapping of the roles of the various goddesses, one triple goddess well-documented in Irish mythology is constantly associated with warfare. This is the formidable and sinister triad of war goddesses, Morrígan, Badb and Macha, sometimes called Nemhain. Sometimes the three are referred to collectively as the Morrígan although each retains her distinctive characteristics.

Morrígan is the Great Queen, who always appears as a very unpleasant woman. In one episode she is described as laughing hatefully as she drowns a prince in the white breakers of the sea.[3] Badb often appears as an ugly hag in a river, washing the armour and weapons of those who are about to die in battle. Macha, the third member of the group, is equally repellant: one reference to her suggests that severed human heads were sacrifically offered in her honour.[4] Many of the sagas suggest a strong association between mortal or part-divine women and death[5] and the origin of this may probably be traced to the roles of the war goddesses.

Two stone carvings of Early Iron Age type may represent this war goddess. The first is the well-known three-faced head from Corleck in

Cavan, which, although usually interpreted as male, could just as well represent a female triple deity. The second is the idol from Lustymore in Fermanagh, which depicts the war goddess as a hag blinded in one eye.[6]

Women Warriors

The role of these war goddesses was to influence the outcome of war, not by engaging in battle, but by magical means and by instilling terror and panic by their presence. However, other goddesses or legendary heroines are described as experts in the *practice* of warfare. There are numerous references to gods and heroes being trained to fight by women, important gods like Lugh and formidable heroes such as Cúchulainn. And the most famous of the warrior queens, Medb (Maeve) — now generally accepted as a goddess in human form — appears as commander of her army, expert in the use of weapons and present in the thick of battle. In one of her battles against Findmor, wife of Celtchar, she is descibed as capturing fifty women after the storming of Dun Sobhairche (Dunseverick, County Antrim).[7]

Because of this strong association of women with warfare in Irish mythology it is interesting to find historical evidence for women warriors in Celtic societies. They existed in Gaul and Britain as well as Ireland. The fighting capabilities of the first-century British queen Boudicca (Boadicea) are well known. Dio Cassius describes her as a powerful warrior wielding a long spear, 'huge of frame, terrifying of aspect and with a harsh voice'.[8] A woman soldier described by Ammianus Marcellinus in fourth-century Gaul rushes to the defence of her husband in battle 'swelling her neck, gnashing her teeth, brandishing her sallow arms of enormous size'. She then proceeds 'to strike blows mingled with kicks, as if they were so many missiles sent from the string of a catapult'.[9] In Ireland this custom of women engaging in battle is documented and must have continued well into the Christian era, for a law promulgated at the end of the seventh century — the Cáin Adomnáin — imposed fines on men who employed women in military operations.[10]

The Evidence from Mythology

Irish mythology only began to be written down in the sixth century although much of it was transcribed at a later date. Scholars are agreed that it contains much pre-Christian social information, but there is no agreement as to the dating of the culture described in these stories.[11] They may reflect society in AD 1000 or 1000 BC or at any time in the intervening two thousand years, so the goddesses referred to in this paper may have been worshipped in the Bronze Age, the Iron Age or the Early Historic period. Indeed it is possible that Irish literature incorporates themes of European origin which may not necessarily reflect realities in

Ireland.

The Evidence from Archaeology

One must turn to archaeology for any evidence of the worship of goddesses in earlier times. In the Neolithic (New Stone) and Early Bronze Ages the Irish archaeological evidence about the nature of religious beliefs is extremely sparse, although reverence for the dead and belief in an after-life can certainly be inferred from the elaborate stone tombs built by the early farmers. Cult centres have also survived in the form of stone circles and circular enclosures of earth and wood. But these tell us little of the actual beliefs of the people. Did they worship a single god or goddess or both? Did they perhaps worship a multiplicity of gods and goddesses?

The motif carved on some of these early stone tombs or passage graves may throw some light on this, although these complex carvings are as difficult to interpret as the evidence from mythology. Some of the angular designs found in Irish passage graves are thought to represent the male form,[12] and two phallic-shaped objects were found during the excavation of passage graves at Knowth.[13] The female form may be represented in Irish and in Breton passage graves by arrangements of spirals, concentric arcs and other curvilinear forms.[14] Not all scholars accept these interpretations, and indeed the carvings are so abstract that it is arguable whether the face or torso of the supposed female form is depicted. To sum up, the archaeological evidence for the worship of actual male or female deities in the Neolithic and Early Bronze Ages is inconclusive. Archaeologists do not at present share the firm belief of the poet John Montague, who sees in the circles carved on the passsage grave of Sesskilgreen in Tyrone homage to an ancient goddess of fertility.[15]

Later Activity Around Passage Graves

While the precise nature of the rites originally performed at passage graves remains unknown, there is some evidence from mythology and tradition that passage graves were regarded with respect long after their original use as burial chambers, and were then frequently, although not exclusively, associated with goddesses. The famous passage grave cemetery in the Boyne valley was the scene for the story of the union of the goddess Boand with the god Dagda.[16] From this union the god Oengus was born and all three deities were said to live in Brúig (or Brú) na Bóinne — the traditional name for Newgrange or for the passage grave cemetery to which it belongs. Knowth passage grave is associated with the goddess Buí or Boí who was wife of the god Lugh, and who may be identical with the goddess Boand.[17] The passage grave at Knocknarea in Sligo is named Miosgán Meadhbha (Maeve's Cairn) after the goddess

Medb, and it is tempting to speculate that the passage grave at Tara, known as the Mound of the Hostages, may also have had a particular association with Medb, who is strongly identified as the sovereign goddess of Tara. Another female deity named Áine, the sun-goddess of Irish mythology, is firmly linked with the passage grave of Knockmany in Tyrone.[18] The name given to the passage grave cemetery at Loughcrew in County Meath — Sliabh na Caillighe (the Hag's Mountain) — refers to the mother goddess in one of her guises as an old hag, which is not unlike the appearance of the war goddess Badb, symbolising her concern with death and decay. The archaeological evidence from one of the passage graves at Loughcrew suggests that it was re-used for burial and possibly as an artist's workshop in the Early Iron Age.[19] While the latter use might suggest disdain for the sanctity of the site, who is to say that the main product of this so-called workshop — decorated and undecorated bone plaques — had not some religious significance?

A possible explanation for this continued reverence for old sacred sites may be that it was deliberately fostered by Celtic or earlier missionaries as a tactful way of converting the native population to belief in a new religion. It is possible that mythological stories of couplings of gods or kings with goddesses may have served a somewhat similar purpose. They may have been an attempt to blend old with new beliefs or to unite different tribal groups by linking their respective deities.

The principal female deity in these stories is the goddess of sovereignty, symbolising the land of Ireland, and in their telling they probably describe the actual pre-Christian inauguration ceremony, in which the prospective king was required to perform the 'banfheis rígi', or marriage of sovereignty, with the goddess of the land to ensure the acceptance of his kingship by its people.[20]

The Female Role in Myth and Society

The preceding exploration of evidence for religious beliefs in prehistoric Ireland leaves many questions unanswered, but it leaves one in no doubt about the powerful roles played by female deities and the high status they enjoyed. It has also been observed that female characters in Irish literature tend to play more active and independent roles than in other literatures of the medieval period.[21] Proinsias Mac Cana explains this by his theory that almost all the heroines of medieval Irish literature are adaptations in human terms of the archetypal female deity. I agree with his view that all the authority and confidence of the goddess is extended in the literature to her human counterpart.

This still leaves open for speculation the much-debated question of whether the image of women in Irish literature, either as goddesses or heroines, affected or reflected the *actual* legal and social status of women. Few would now agree with the views of Eoin MacNeill, who believed that mythology proved the existence in Ireland of a matrilinear system of succession of rulers.[22] On the other hand, if one were to accept the analogy of the cult of the Virgin Mary and the corresponding poor status of women in Catholic countries,[23] one would be dubious about the status of women in early Ireland being mirrored in or receiving any beneficial effect from the powerful portrayals of goddesses and heroines in literature. The high status of St Brigid is exceptional and hardly affects the validity of Marina Warner's conclusion that 'there is no logical equivalence in any society between exalted female objects of worship and a high position for women'.[24]

The difficulties of relating Irish mythology to a precise period in time have already been mentioned. But we must assume that mythology evolved over a long time and so we should be able to detect in it evidence of changing beliefs. For example, there are hints that some goddesses were worshipped in Ireland longer than gods. Danu, described in Cormac's glossary as the mother of Irish gods, may be one of these early goddesses. She is commemorated in the name of the Irish gods, the Tuatha Dé Danann, or descendants of the goddess Danu. Does this reflect another attempt to mingle old with new beliefs? Is it another example of deference being paid to the established goddess by followers of the new religion? The same kind of interpretation could be given to an episode recounted in the Leabhar Gabhála — the Book of Invasions — when three goddesses, Ériu, Banbha and Fódla, confront the sons of Míl, the new invaders, accompanied by their druids. Eventually the goddesses are appeased and accept the new arrivals.

Women in Christian Times

When Christianity was introduced in the fifth century AD, the pagan deities were not displaced overnight. The kind of tolerance which I have suggested was shown by earlier faiths was undoubtedly a policy of Christian missionaries in Ireland, who, where possible, adapted the old beliefs to the new creed. Attributes and functions of pagan deities were allocated to saints. Holy wells dedicated to saints, often female saints, replaced the sacred wells of the pagan deities. However, not all deities could be so easily transformed. The difficulty of giving a Christian meaning to the war goddess must explain why the powerful goddess Badb reappears in folk tradition as the shadowy, mysterious *bean sí (banshee)*.

Brigid

Perhaps the most remarkable adaptation was the transformation of the goddess Brigit or Brigid, a pan-Celtic deity and also a triple goddess, into a Christian saint. St Brigid's feast-day is 1 February, the same day as Imbolc, the great spring festival of the pagan year. An account of the goddess in Cormac's Glossary associates her with healing, smithcraft and learning.[25] The saint too is concerned with healing and is the patron of poets and men of learning. Moreover, Giraldus Cambrensis in the twelfth century describes how a sacred flame burns perpetually at Brigid's monastery at Kildare — a mysterious fire tended by nineteen virgins and surrounded by a magic enclosure.[26] Notwithstanding the unreliability of Cambrensis as a commentator, several writers have interpreted this perpetual fire, probably correctly, as a survival of a pagan fire cult.[27]

Fire Cults

A fire cult may also have taken place at another ceremonial site, the hill-top of Knockaulin, which is five miles from Kildare and is identified with the royal site of Dun Áilinne. Evidence from recent excavations has prompted the suggestion that ceremonials involving fire and feasting took place there during the Iron Age.[28] References to perpetual fires at the monasteries of Seirkieran, Kilmainham and Inishmurray suggest that fire cults may have been widespread in Ireland.[29] The place-name for Kildare — Cell dara — is a further indication of a pagan sanctuary, the name Cell dara being thought to derive from a sacred oak tree.[30]

Women and Monasteries

The unusually high status of St Brigid and the success of her monastery may be largely due to the pagan origins of both the saint and the site. A seventh-century account of Kildare by Cogitosus describes it as a very large double establishment of clerics and nuns ruled jointly by a bishop and an abbess, but, and this is very unusual, with the abbess taking precedence over the bishop. A successful monastery required adequate endowments. It would have been an advantage to site a monastery on a pagan sanctuary, for the lands which must have been endowed to the sanctuary could have been more easily transferred to representatives of the new faith than other property. The lack of success of many of the early Church foundations organised on diocesan rather than monastic lines has been attributed to the Irish property-holding system, which in practice meant that land could not be given to the Church without the consent of the whole kin group. The laws relating to the inheritance of land can certainly be blamed for the scarcity of women's religious houses in Early Christian Ireland.[31] Only in exceptional circumstances could a woman inherit land, and even then she only held a life interest in it. Most convents probably suffered from an absence of such perpetual endowments and many communities must have broken up upon the death of their foundress. It is against this background that one must judge the considerable importance of those convents which survived and flourished — monasteries like Clonbroney founded by St Samthann, Killeedy founded by St Ite, St Monenna's convent at Killeevy and St Gobnait's at

Ballyvourney.

Sometimes women were allowed to take up the religious life in the normal monastery. But a woman applying to join St Senan's monastery on Scattery Island was admitted only after a strong protest from her at the saint's unwillingness to let her in: 'Christ came to save women no less than men. He suffered for the sake of women no less than for men. Women have given service and ministry to Christ and his apostles. Women enter the heavenly kingdom no less than men.'[32] Frequently churches especially for women were built close to normal monasteries as at Glendalough, Clonmacnoise, Inchcleraun, Inishglora and Inishmurray.[33]

The rights of women regarding the inheritance of property remained limited throughout the Early Historic period. However, in other legal matters they progressed fairly rapidly from a position of having no independent legal capacity in the sixth and early seventh centuries to one of near equality with men by the late seventh and early eighth centuries.[34] The influence of the Church probably contributed to this improvement and, in some cases, the Church appears to have benefited from the higher legal status of women. It now became possible for a woman to bequeath as a gift to the Church the 'produce of her two hands', without first requiring her husband's permission.[35]

The typical monastery in Early Christian Ireland, far from being remote from the world, was the centre of community life where women and children must have had a place. The lay people who worked the land for the monks were usually married and some of the clergy were also married, their sons often succeeding them in ecclesiastical appointments. However, a common feature in the eighth and ninth centuries was the presence, either adjacent to the monastery or within its precincts, of groups of ascetics who led chaste, austere and devout lives very much in the tradition of the early eremitical Church. Can one attribute to these groups and to the many contemporary reformers the emergence of an attitude which viewed women as 'seductresses, temptresses and the cause of man's downfall'?[36] This extreme view, while in keeping with the Church's fear of sexuality, owes much, as Margaret MacCurtain has suggested, to a preoccupation with male chastity. Its origins may go back to the practice of Syneisactism in the early Church — men and women living chastely together. It would appear that this practice came to be regarded as a test of male rather than female chastity. This view of women, widespread throughout the Christian world, can be traced in many of the Irish documentary sources, in a number of saints' lives, in the calendar of saints known as the Martyrology of Oengus and in several early poems.[37] A recurrent theme in lives of saints is of them fleeing from the sound of cows and sheep because of the danger of meeting the women minding the herds, for in the overwhelming logic of words attributed to St Kevin, 'where there are cows there are women, where there are women there is sin, where there is sin there is the Devil, and where there is the Devil there is Hell'.[38]

The Image of the Sinful Woman

The same view of women is almost certainly reflected in the popularity of the subject of Adam and Eve on the stone High Crosses. A reading of the poem 'Eve's Lament' helps one to imagine the kind of sermon these carvings of the fall of man might have illustrated. In this late tenth- or early eleventh-century poem Eve, and by implication all womankind, is clearly blamed for all the misfortunes of the human race:

> I am Eve, great Adam's wife
> 'Tis I that outraged Jesus of old;
> 'Tis I that robbed my children of Heaven,
> By rights 'tis I that should have gone upon the cross.
>
> 'Tis I that plucked the apple,
> Which went across my gullet:
> So long as they endure in the light of day,
> So long women will not cease from folly.
>
> There would be no ice in any place,
> There would be no glistening windy winter,
> There would be no hell, there would be no sorrow,
> There would be no fear, if it were not for me.[39]

This view of sinful woman is reaffirmed in a very significant carving on another High Cross — Muiredach's cross at Monasterboice. In the judgement scene there appears among the damned a straddled woman clearly expressing her sexuality, portraying the sin of lust, and being firmly directed towards hell.[40] Another interesting carving of the same kind is the partly clothed figure on White Island in Fermanagh. It is an enigmatic statue, almost certainly representing a female, and is quite different from the five other ecclesiastical statues found at the same monastery. It could be interpreted as an illustration of the seductive powers of women and a reminder to both monks and laity of the dangers of the flesh.

In the light of such thinking, it is not surprising to find considerable segregation of the sexes in the early Church — separate convents, separate places of worship, and sometimes, as at Kildare, separate areas within the monastic church. This distrust of women was even carried beyond the grave, as, for example, in the island monastery of Inishmurray and at Carrickmore in County Tyrone, where men and women had separate burial grounds. St Colmcille is supposed to have insisted that women of ill repute should be buried out of earshot of his bell.

Cult of the Virgin Mary

While Eve symbolised the spirit of evil, the way of sin and death, Mary, through her Immaculate Conception and the virgin birth, became the paragon, showing the way to paradise and salvation. Poems, hymns, relics and litanies point to the existence of a cult of the Virgin Mary in Ireland from the eighth century onwards.[41] While the influence of classical mythology has been noted in certain aspects of the Marian cult,[42] in Ireland the cult seems totally orthodox, and, unlike the devotion to St Brigid, it does not appear to have assimilated local pagan beliefs. Surprisingly, Mary rarely appears in the surviving art of the Early Historic period. Apart from her presence in scriptural scenes like the flight into Egypt, she is seldom depicted on High Crosses. She is never shown in crucifixion scenes, and the well-known full-page portrait of the virgin and child in the Book of Kells is quite exceptional.

The late tenth century saw the beginnings of an upsurge of popular devotion to the Virgin Mary, not only in Ireland but throughout Western Europe, which continued during the following centuries and was greatly assisted by men like St Bernard, founder of the Cistercians. In southern France it coincided with the appearance of courtly love poetry, and eventually, after the Albigensian Crusade of the early thirteenth century, a remarkable fusion occurred between these two disparate traditions, with Mary taking on the mantle of the poets' love object, and the poets being converted to the Christian sexual ethic.[43]

Romanesque Carvings

In the eleventh and twelfth centuries one of the methods of teaching this Christian ethic was through figures carved on the new Romanesque churches built in France. Judging from these carvings the sins most condemned at this time were those of lust and avarice. Similar carvings, but confined to representing lust, soon appeared in Ireland. In France lust was represented in many forms; in Ireland it was mainly illustrated by exhibitionist figures, with female examples far outnumbering male. This is hardly surprising in view of the long-established Irish attitude which regarded woman as the main cause of the sin. French Romanesque architecture had a strong influence on the Irish Romanesque style and the Irish exhibitionists clearly derive from French examples.[44]

One of the earliest Irish female exhibitionists is carved on the chancel arch of the Romanesque Nun's Church at Clonmacnoise which can be dated to about AD 1166.[45] Its discreet genital display is typical of the Irish Romanesque period; a rather mild reminder of the sin of lust. A more forceful condemnation is expressed by the exhibitionists found on English Romanesque churches of the same period where the vulva is frequently shown in a grotesque and exaggerated way.

Sheela-na-gigs

This kind of gross emphasis of genitalia does not appear in Ireland until the fifteenth and sixteenth centuries when female exhibitionists known as Sheela-na-gigs were carved on the walls of castles as well as churches. They were no longer placed in a decorative architectural setting as on the Romanesque churches but were set in isolation above doors and windows or on quoins, frequently almost out of sight on the upper wall levels. Their presence on castles suggests that these repulsive carvings now held a significance other than their original moral one.

This study of women in early Ireland began with the power exerted by female deities in pre-Christian Ireland. Their association with war and death, with victories and defeats, probably led to the evolution of overt genital display as a dominant weapon, such as was used by women on several occasions to subdue Cúchulainn, according to the Táin and other sagas.[46] Christian reformers later used the latent power of sexual symbolism in a mildly reprimanding way to curb sexual immorality among men, reviving in them the ancient fear of women. The study ends with the power that stone carvings of the naked woman were believed to exert in late Medieval Ireland: a time when man, if he had survived the terrible devastation of the Black Death in the mid-fourteenth century, was preoccupied with the uncertainty of life and dread of evil powers. This ultimately caused men to set images of blatant female sexuality on their castles and churches, probably in the hope that this would give protection from destructive forces against which they were powerless.

Notes

1   H. Wagner, 'Origins of Pagan Irish Religion and the Study of Names', in *Bulletin of the Ulster Place-name Society*, 2 (1979), 25-6.
2   A. Ross, *Pagan Celtic Britain*, 1967, 20-2, 366.
3   M. Dillon and N.K. Chadwick, *The Celtic Realms*, 1967, 144.
4   Ross, 95.
5   M. Ní Bhrolcháin, 'Women in Early Irish Myths and Sagas', *The Crane Bag* 4, 1 (1980), 16-18.
6   H. Hickey, *Images of Stone*, 1976, 21, 30.
7   T. Kinsella (trans), *The Tain*, 1979, 126-7.
8   Dillon and Chadwick, 27.
9   *Ibid.*, 154.
10 J. Ryan, 'The Cáin Adomnáin', in *Studies in Early Irish Law*, Royal Irish Academy, 1936, 269-76.
11 R. Warner, 'The Archaeology of Historic Sites', in *Bulletin of the Ulster Place-name Society* 2 (1979), 43.
12 M. Herity, *Irish Passage Graves*, 1974, 103-6.
13 G. Eogan, 'Excavations at Knowth, Co. Meath', in *Proc. R. Ir. Acad.* 74C (1974), 47, fig 16 (object of antler or bone). The second object is of stone and is illustrated in *Ireland Today* 993 (Nov/Dec. 1982), 4.

Carved Figure, White Island, Fermanagh (photograph, Ulster Museum)

14   Herity, 103-6.
15   J. Montague, *A Slow Dance*, 1975, 11.
16   P. MacCana, *Celtic Mythology*, 1970, 33.
17   F.J. Byrne, Historical Note on Cnogba (Knowth) in *Proc. R. Ir. Acad.* 66C (1968), 386; and Wagner, 26.
18   M.A. Killanin and M.V. Duignan, *The Shell Guide to Ireland*, 1967, 78.
19   E. Evans, *Prehistoric and Early Christian Ireland, a Guide*, 1966, 170-2.
20   P. MacCanaa, 'Women in Irish Mythology', *The Crane Bag* 4, 1 (1980), 7-11.
21   *Ibid.*, 9-10.
22   E. MacNeill, *Early Irish Laws and Institutions*, 1935, 64-7.
23   M. Warner, *Alone of all her sex. The Myth and the Cult of the Virgin Mary*, 1978, 284.
24   *Ibid.*, 283.
25   J.F. Kenney, *The Sources for the Early History of Ireland*, 1979, 357-8.
26   J.J. O'Meara (trans), *Topography of Ireland*, 1951, XXXIV-XXXVI.
27   Kenney, 357.
28   B. Wailes, 'Dun Ailinne: an interim report', in D.W. Harding (ed.), *Hillforts*, 1976, 229-331.
29   K. Hughes and A. Hamlin, *The Modern Traveller to the Early Irish Church*, 1977, 30. I should like to record my indebtedness to Dr Ann Hamlin for drawing my attention to many aspects relating to women in the early Irish Church.
30   Kenney, 358.
31   *Ibid.*
32   Hughes and Hamlin, 8.
33   *Ibid.*, 68-9.
34   D. Ó Corráin, 'Women in Early Irish Society', in *Women in Irish Society*, MacCurtain and O Corráin (eds), 1978, 1-13.
35   D.A. Binchy, 'The Legal Capacity of Women in regard to Contracts', in *Studies in Early Irish Law*, Binchy (ed.), 1936, 275-6.
36   M. MacCurtain, 'Towards an Appraisal of the Religious Image of Women', *The Crane Bag* 4, 1 (1980), 27-8.
37   *Ibid.*
38   I am grateful to Dr Katharine Simms for drawing my attention to this reference from the medieval life of St Kevin.
39   K. Meyer, *Ancient Irish Poetry*, 1913, 34.
40   A. Weir, 'Three Carved Figures in County Louth', *J. Co. Louth Arch. and Hist. Soc.* 19, 1 (1977), 67-8, Pl. 2A.
41   P. O'Dwyer, *Devotion to Mary in Ireland, 700-1100*, 1976.
42   Warner, 34-6.
43   *Ibid.*, 130-48.
44   J. Anderson, *The Witch on the Wall*, 1977, chap. IV.
45   *Ibid.*, 39, figs 14 and 15.
46   Cross and Slover, *Ancient Irish Tales*, 1969, 151, 237.

The Supernatural Wailing Woman

Patricia Lysaght

1

A great variety of traditions concerning a solitary, crying, female super-natural being connected with deaths[1] in certain families, and popularly known as the banshee, is found over the whole of mainland Ireland.[2] In this essay the wailing aspect, the aural manifestation is examined.[3]

The examination is based on the archival material in the Manuscript Archive of the Department of Irish Folklore, University College Dublin.[4] Due to the abundance and prevalence of this source material it is possible to establish what is generally told and believed about the being in Ireland.

Before dealing in detail with the aural manifestation of the being I propose to briefly survey the names by which she is known as some of these describe her role behaviour — her keening or wailing — and may also have influenced ideas about her character and the quality of her cry in certain areas.

In addition to banshee, *bean sí*, the best known name for the being which occurs over the whole distribution area of the belief, a number of less common names are also found. The term *bean chaointe*,[5] 'keening woman' occurs in parts of Counties Limerick and Tipperary in Munster and north-west County Mayo in Connacht. It aptly describes aspects of her appearance and behaviour and it appears that many traits in the traditions about her are best explained by assuming that her appearance and actions mirror to some extent those of human keening women. The infrequent occurrence of the term is probably due to the established use of the same term for the human female keener.

A group of names (incorporating *badhb, babha, bo(bó) chaointe* and *bo chaointeacháin*) may be designated the *badhbh*-appellations[6] and has a distinct distribution area in south-east Ireland which is here referred to as the *badhbh*-area. *Badhb*, 'bibe', is found in County Waterford and in south Counties Kilkenny and Tipperary, areas with close dialectical affinity with Waterford Irish. *Babha*, 'bow', occurs mainly in County Wexford but the term has also seeped into north-east County Kilkenny and south-east County Kildare. On the periphery of these areas are found the 'derivatory' terms *bo(bó) chaointe*[7] (mid and south Tipperary) and *bo chaointeacháin*[8] (south Kilkenny), the attributive genitive *chaointe* and *chaointeacháin* clarifying, as it were, the kind of *badhb* or *baba* being dealt with.[9]

In view of the variety of names for the being that generic term 'supernatural death-messenger' is used in this essay. It stresses her principal activity — proclaiming deaths which are imminent or have just occurred.

2

From the discussion of the appellations it is already evident that crying or keening is an important characteristic of the being. An aural manifestation is, in fact, a basic element of the supernatural death-messenger belief in Ireland and it is a *sine qua non* in a death situation.

The sound is described by a variety of terms in English and Irish. Some of the terms are found all over Ireland, others are confined to a limited area, and still others have only been recorded once and may possibly have no foundation in collective tradition.

The commonest term is *cry*. There are examples of this term in my material from all over Ireland, but the term seems to have been especially common in Leinster. The synonymous Irish term *gol*, 'crying', 'weeping', has also been recorded.[10] It is found in Tipperary and Cork and is most common in Kerry.

The next most common in term is *wail*.[11] It is more prominent in Munster and Leinster than in Connacht and Ulster.

The term *lament* recorded from Leinster, Munster and Ulster is not very common.[12] In Munster (Cork and Kerry) we find the synonymous Irish term *olagón*.[13] In County Waterford the term *ochón* has been recorded once. Like *olagón* this is associated with the performance of keening women at wakes and funerals.

Still another Irish term with the meaning 'cry', 'wail', or 'lament', namely *lóg*, is found in Waterford and the form *lógóireacht*, 'crying', 'wailing', has been recorded in Galway.

The term *caoineadh* is the third most common term and it has been recorded from all the four provinces. It seems to be the most popular in Munster (Cork, Kerry, Tippeary and Waterford). There are also additional examples of the anglicised form *keen*.[14]

Other terms found are *moan* (six examples), *roar* (eight examples), *scream* (seven examples), *shriek* (four examples), *screech* (one example), *call* (three examples). Irish terms are *glaoch* meaning 'call', *béic*, 'shout', 'yell' (three examples), *scréach*, 'screech', 'scream' (one example).

It is apparent that there is great variety in the terms used to describe the sound through which the being makes her presence known. No single county has less than two terms. The greatest variation, however, is found in what we have referred to above as the *badhbh* area, i.e. the south-eastern counties. Thus there are six different terms in Carlow, seven in

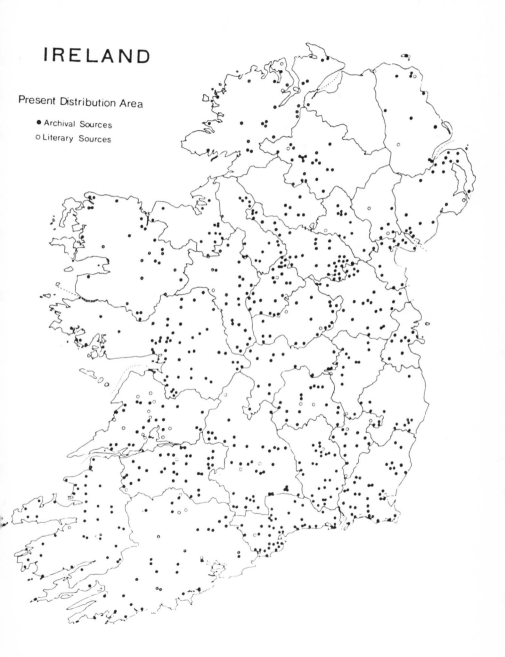

IRELAND

Present Distribution Area

• Archival Sources
○ Literary Sources

Wexford, eight in Tipperary and no less than thirteen in Waterford. From the point of view of their meaning, the terms would seem to fall into two main groups, though the dividing lines cannot always be drawn with absolute precision. Sorrow and grief are the key elements in many of the terms found over the greater part of Ireland. The terms *wail, lament, olagón, lóg, caoineadh* (keen) are clear-cut examples of such terms. That the term *cry* in the majority of the instances has the meaning 'weeping' rather than 'shouting' is evident from the contexts and the frequency with which it corresponds to *gol* in areas where Irish still survives. Many of these terms not only express sorrow in general, but could also more particularly refer to the mourning or the mourning sounds made by keening women at wakes and funerals, and there is, as already indicated, little doubt that the supernatural death-messenger should be considered as a supernatural counterpart of such human mourners to some extent. The terms in the first group would also indicate that the supernatural being is sympathetic towards the person on the occasion of whose death she makes her presence known and that she shares the grief of relatives and friends. Her behaviour is thus non-violent and human.

The second group of terms expresses a more fierce and frightening side of the being. In this group may be included *roar, scream, shriek, screech, scréach* and *béic*, terms connoting loud, sharp, shrill or piercing qualities. Such sounds were not lacking in the performances of the human keeners. They are, indeed, referred to by observers of real keening performances — especially by those who were opposed to the custom.[15] Nevertheless, these terms are also suggestive of the human sphere. They can be used to denote the sound of wild animals and dangerous and hostile supernatural beings. It is noteworthy that the terms are mainly found in the *badhbh*-area. The image of an aggressive and threatening being would seem to be stronger there than elsewhere in Ireland.

The *caoineadh* performed by professional or semi-professional mourners often included improvised verses, in which the deceased was praised and the sorrow of the survivors expressed. But it is clear that the parallelism between the 'real' keening and the keening of the supernatural death-messenger, does not go this far. A few records mention wailing exclamatory phrases such as *och, ochón* and 'wirra, wirra'.[16] Meaningful words are referred to in one record only where the hearer was supposed to imagine some form of words in the cry — the Christian name of the person who was called away.[17] The particular motif that the being calls out the name of the person about to die is not found explicitly stated in other archival sources.[18] It would appear to lack deeper roots in genuine folk belief and does not form part of the collective tradition in any area. On the other hand, the idea that hearing one's name inexplicably called out is a death-omen, is not infrequently met with — though not in combination witht he supernatural death-messenger.

Traditional records give an idea of the character of the sound emitted by the supernatural death-messenger through the terms they employ for it and through many direct and detailed descriptions of its particular qualities. Many of these motifs are what scholars term *criterion motifs*; their function is to prove the experience encountered could not possibly have a natural explanation.

The records often stress that the sound had special connections with sorrow and bereavement, 'mournful', 'lonesome' and 'sad', being the adjectives most frequently used.

Another way to 'prove' the experience was of a supernatural kind is to compare the sound to something which used to exist but no longer does. Of special interest in this connection are the comparisons with the keening women of former times. Such comparisons are mainly found in the western counties where the practice of keening continued until the turn of the century.[19] On the whole the stress on the mournfulness and sadness of her cry is also much stronger in the west, and especially in Munster, than in the east.

Apart from the comparisons with human keeners there are also comparisons with ordinary women in sorrow or distress. Some of the examples should, perhaps, be seen against the background of an origin explanation that the supernatural death-messenger used to be a member of the family for which she cries.[20]

The opinion that she sounds like a crying child is fairly widespread. Again it is possible that there is a certain amount of affinity between the idea that the being *sounds like* a child and that she *originated from* a particular prematurely deceased child of the family for which she 'cries'. The complex of beliefs surrounding the banshee and her kin is bordering on, and has been influenced by, the beliefs about children who have died without baptism. In Irish tradition, as elsewhere, such children who have not had the benefit of the appropriate rites to incorporate them into the community are thought to be restless and express their distress through crying and wailing.[21]

Another major group of comparisons is drawn from the sounds of animals and birds, especially those with nocturnal habits. The cry of cats is the most frequently mentioned. More specifically, the comparison would appear to have its background in the similarity between wailing and mourning and the nocturnal cry of mating cats. Though similar to this sound, the being's cry could nevertheless be distinguished from it according to the tradition bearers. In Waterford we find this opinion expressed in a proverbial saying: *Ní bhíonn aon lóg cathach age 'n chat mar a bhíonn age 'n bhaidhb* (The cat has no sorrowful cry like the *badhb* has).[22]

The howling of dogs, especially at night, is commonly considered to be a death-omen in Irish tradition, as well as in many other countries. The tradition of the dogs associated with the O'Keeffe family (*gaidhríní Uí Chaoimh*) is especially well known. In view of this it is not surprising the supernatural death-messenger's cry should be compared with a dog's howl. What is noteworthy is rather that this trait is comparatively scarce.

Though similar to the howl of a dog, nevertheless, her wail was, according to tradition bearers, clearly distinguishable from it.

The cry is also compared with the cry of the vixen in a few records from Leinster. Here too, however, while acknowledging the similarity of the sounds, tradition bearers also stress the recognisable differences, between them.

Comparison with the scream of a hare caught in a trap, a very piercing and pitiful sound, is somewhat surprisingly, only found once in the source material.

Comparisons with bird sounds are far scarcer than comparisons with animal sounds. In spite of its nocturnal habits and its ominous character the owl has only invited comparison with the supernatural death-messenger once.[23] There it is said she sounded like the *scréachán reilige*, literally 'the graveyard screecher', i.e. the screech or barn owl.[24] The sound of the *gabhairín reo*, 'the jack snipe',[25] is said to be similar to the cry of the supernatural death-messenger in three Kerry records. This bird, which frequents solitary localities like bogs and marshes, makes an eerie drumming sound with its wings when descending in the air. Thus it appears that comparisons between the being's cry and bird sounds are not part of the collective tradition except possibly in Kerry and then only with the jack snipe. It is especially noteworthy that such comparisons are totally absent in the *badhbh*-area.[26]

In certain printed sources the cry is likened to the sound of the wind or a storm.[27] Only once is something comparable found in the archival material where the wind is compared to the supernatural death-messenger rather than vice-versa.[28] The style is also contrived and atypical of oral rendering. There can be little doubt that the wind-simile is a literary device without footing in a genuine folk tradition.

Further criteria of the supernatural origin of the sound used by tradition bearers are additional qualities of a kind totally foreign to the sounds of humans or animals. The extremely loud volume of the sound which 'filled the whole vault of the heavens' is stressed in a number of records. It is not surprising then to find it said that it could be heard a long distance away, that it permeates buildings and that the whole ground in the vicinity shakes and that even the deaf could hear it.

The extraordinary duration of the cry is also stressed in records from east Munster, Leinster and south Ulster. This quality of the sound will of course also 'prove' that it could not have a natural cause.

A more firmly established tradition, however, is that the cry was heard a specified number of times. The tradition most commonly met with is that the cry is heard three times. This motif is especially common in Waterford, in Munster, and it also occurs in Leinster (Kilkenny, Longford, Louth, Meath, Westmeath, Wexford and Wicklow). Outside this area only three isolated examples of this motif have been found.[29] Repetition in three is, of course, commonly met with in connection with magic and the supernatural, but in relation to the wail of the death-messenger, the south-easterly concentration of the motif would hardly appear to be incidental. The distribution pattern rather gives us the impression that the trait was originally attached to the *badhbh* in Waterford and spread from there eastwards and northwards. It is noteworthy that the three cries are frequently met with in *memorates* — a term coined by C.W. von Sydow to denote narratives of personal happenings[30] — from Waterford, and that they are there used to test the reality of the experience at its very occurrence as shown in the following example:[31]

Thuit seo amach i mí Lúnasa 1913. Bhíos im'thig féin i mBaile an Gambóna agus an t-am idir an dá sholas sa tráthnóna. D'airíos an bhéic is uaigní do bhuail riamh ar mo chluasa. Mheasas go raibh an glór sin tuairim is dhá chéad slat thíos an bhóthair ón dtigh. Bhíos ag brath go dtiocfadh ceann eile agus, gan morán moille, tháinig, agus timpeall an fhad céanna ar an dtaobh eile den tigh. Bhíos agus mo chluasa ar tinneall agam ag feitheamh leis an tríú béic. Nuair a tháinig, chuir sí crith millteach im'bhalla uile.

Ba shin an méid, ach ar maidin bhí comharsa béaldorais ar an gclár dá thórramh. Colbárd a b'ainm den duine seo agus nuair a d'innis mé mo scéal bhí sé i mbéal gach duine go mbíodh an bhadhbh riamh agus i gcónaí i ndiaidh na treibhe sin — Colbert. This occurred in August 1913. I was in my own house in Baile an Gambóna at twilight. I heard the most lonesome screech that ever hit my ears. I judged that the sound was about two hundred yards down the road from the house. I was expecting that another one would come and it did come without much delay and it was about the same distance at the other side of the house. I had my ears cocked waiting for the third shout. When it came it made every member of my body shake terribly.

That was all, but in the morning a next-door neighbour was being waked. His name was Colbert. When I told my story everybody said that the *badhbh* ever and always used to follow that family — Colbert.

Another interesting trait is that her cry will stop at command. There are five clear-cut examples from the archival source material and they stem from Mayo, Roscommon and Sligo in Connacht and from the adjacent Leinster counties of Longford and Westmeath, e.g.:

. . . if you say 'stop!' and listen you won't hear no more; 'stop!' and you won't hear another sound.[32]

The only printed source referring to the belief, Mac Giollarnáth,[33] (from Iorrus Aithneach, County Galway) contains a curious variation, namely that the death-messenger will do the opposite of what you tell her to do:

Éist, éist![34] i.e. *bí i do thos. Deirtear nach cóir 'éist!' a rá nuair a cloistear an bhean sidhe, ach má abruighthear 'éist!' leanfaidh sí do'n chaoineachán.*

(Stop! stop! i.e. be silent! It is said that it is not right to say 'be silent' when the banshee is heard for if it is said she will continue crying.)

It is difficult to say whether this form of the motif is traditional or an individual invention. The idea that things are inverse in the supernatural sphere is a common one, and the refusal of the death messenger to obey the command of a mortal gives her the image of a proud and mighty being, at the same time as humans can find comfort in the thought that she can be outwitted. Whatever the solution of this particular problem may be, it is clear that the silencing motif here, in both its forms, fulfils the role of a criterion motif.

Yet another criterion motif with a northerly distribution (Cavan, Down, Longford and Mayo) describes the sound as inaudible to some people though very clearly audible to others. Sometimes only one person in a particular gathering or crowd will hear the sound.

A great variety of criterion motifs are connected with the directions from which the sound is heard and how it moves. A few records from Cork and Tipperary state that the sound can be heard from all directions simultaneously. More frequently we meet with the idea that the sound has got an elusive quality which makes it impossible to pin down the place it comes from or that it keeps coming from different directions at extremely short intervals. Alternatively it is said that the sound keeps moving away as one tries to approach it.

The extraordinary speed at which the sound is imagined to travel is very frequently stressed in the material and people obviously regarded it as one of the main characteristics of the sound.

Another sure indication the sound is emanating from the supernatural death-messenger, is that it is heading for, encircling or leaving the house of a sick or dying person. As might be expected, the being most commonly makes her presence known at or near the house of the person who is about to die. No doubt it is to be imagined that the sound is getting gradually louder as it approaches and that if fades away once it has passed the house in which the dying person dwells. Sometimes it is said that the sound started high up in the air and gradually descended upon the house for which it is heading. A number of records also state that the sound encircles the house. Contrary to what one might have expected, it is nowhere indicated in any source, archival or printed, whether the encircling was withershins or sunwise, *tuathal* or *deiseal*.

Records from Connacht, Munster and Ulster indicate that the cry would follow the course of a stream or river. The explanation for this may be that sounds, particularly in the stillness of the night, would carry along or across water. In one solitary Kerry record it is mentioned that the cry always goes against the stream. This, like the idea that the banshee would continue to cry if she was told to stop, would seem to be based on the idea that things are happening in a reverse manner in the supernatural sphere.

In a few scattered examples from different parts of Ireland a sound is identified as emanating from the supernatural death-messenger because it heads for the house of the dying person and goes on from there to the graveyard. This trait, however, does not seem to have been firmly established in the collective tradition of any particular area.

The effects of the sound on those who hear it exemplify another set of criterion motifs. Apart from the abundant general statements indicating that the cry was frightening, we find a number of sources telling of tangible physical effects upon humans who heard it, e.g. 'getting on your nerves' or bringing 'the cold sweat out on you'. An expression commonly used in connection with the fear experienced when the cry was heard is 'it would put the hair standing on your head'. It is likely that most informants have taken this phrase quite literally.

The fright the cry would give animals would also 'prove' the genuineness of the phenomenon, in particular when the animals were types commonly believed to possess occult hearing and ability to distinguish between the natural and the supernatural. Dogs, frequently credited with the ability of seeing and hearing ghosts,[35] and often found in or in the near vicinity of houses, and also, perhaps, sometimes especially attached to the person about to die, are mentioned. Fright or panic in horses confronted with the cry is only met with twice in the source material, although horses are otherwise thought to be just as skilled in spotting supernatural beings as dogs.[36] The reason they are seldom mentioned in connection with the banshee and her kin may be that their behaviour would be less easily observed by people inside or in the vicinity of a house. There is one isolated account of sheep refusing to pass a spot where a sound attributed to the death-messenger was reported to have been heard.

While there is motley variation in the descriptions of the cry and in the motifs used to 'prove' or make plausible the genuineness of the supernatural experiences, it may be said that the common factor in many of the most frequent traits is a death in a particular family.

Notes

1 The main exceptions to this rule take the form of legends which are based on the belief that it is wrong or even dangerous to interfere with or insult the being. These legends deal with activities of the being which are peripheral to her ordinary role as an announcer of death. See also note 3.

2 So far I have not found any definite evidence of the belief in Tory Island or in the Aran Islands, areas where a fair amount of collecting was done. The belief also apparently lacked importance in Scattery Island off the south coast of County Clare. See also note 3.

3 The main traits in the traditions of the being (including those referred to in notes 1, 2), are dealt with in detail in Patricia Lysaght, *The Banshee*, Dub-

lín 1985.

4   This material consists of the traditional information in the Main Manuscripts Collection (IFC) dating from the late 1920's and the Schools' Manuscripts Collection (IFCS), 1937-38. It also includes the results of the *Banshee Questionnaire* circulated by the Department of Irish Folklore in 1976 (see *Béaloideas* 42-4, 1974-6, 88-93 for the English version of the questionnaire), and the author's fieldwork 1976-8.

5   And similar forms, e.g., *bean chaoint'* and *bean a chaointe*.

6   See Niall Ó Dónaill, *Foclóir Gaeilge-Béarla*, Baile Átha Cliath 1977, under *badhbh*. We may note here that the meanings 'a royston-crow, a vulture or other ravenous bird, carrion-crow' given to *badhbh* in Dinneen's and Ó Dónaill's dictionaries are not, so far as I have been able to ascertain, found anywhere in living speech in Ireland, and it would appear that they have been taken over from the old literary texts.

7   Also spelled *boheente, bohaíonta, boheantar, bohinkey* and *bohynta* in the archival material; *boheentha* in St. John D. Seymour and H.L. Neligan, *True Irish Ghost Stories*, London 1914, 198 and *bocheentha* in John Banim, *Tales, By The O'Hara Family*, London 1825, 64.

8   Also spelled *boheentacán* and *bocaoideachán* in the archival material.

9   There are also indications that a further term *bochaointeach*, possibly a variant form of *bo chaointeacháin*, may have been used on the southern verge of the *bo chaointe, bo chaointeacháin* areas (in Kilcash, County Tipperary and in Glen, County Carlow), but it now appears to have fallen into disuse.

10   There are 266 examples of *cry* in the material I have investigated and 110 of these are from Leinster. There are also twelve examples of *gol*.

11   Fifty-four records from twenty-three counties.

12   Fourteen records from eleven counties.

13   Three examples. This term also occurs in a Donegal questionnaire reply, but it is possible that the informant has been influenced by the Irish version of the Banshee Questionnaire (which included the word *olagón*) which he had used.

14   Thirty-two records of *caoineadh* and eighteen examples of *keen*.

15   Seán Ó Súilleabháin, *Irish Wake Amusements*, Cork 1967, 136-43; Diarmaid Ó Muirithe, 'An Chaointeoireacht in Éirinn — Tuairiscí na dTaistealaithe', *Gnéithe den Chaointeoireacht*, Breandán Ó Madagáin (eag.), Baile Átha Cliath 1978, 20-9.

16   This is no doubt 'A Mhuire, 'Mhuire' (Mary, Mary!, referring to the Blessed Virgin).

17   This is a questionnaire reply from An Ceathrú Rua, County Galway.

18   I have found the motif in one literary source — T. Crofton Croker, *Fairy Legends and Traditions of the South of Ireland*, London 1826, 201.

19   Ó Súilleabháin, 143.

20   Tradition bearers sometimes explain the connection between the supernatural death-messenger and the families she follows by saying that she is a dead member of the family in question.

21   See note 25 above. For the position of these children in Nordic tradition see Juha Pentikäinen: *The Nordic Dead-Child Tradition*, FF Communications No. 202, Helsinki 1968; for their state in Irish tradition see Anne O'Connor, 'Unbaptised Children in Irish Tradition' (unpublished) UCD, 1978, 'The Placeless Dead', *Sinsear* 1979, 33-41 and 'The Death and Burial of Unbaptised Children in Irish Folk Tradition', unpublished Thesis, UCD, 1981. The connecting link between such children and the supernatural death-messenger has undoubtedly been the cry.

22   R.B. Breatnach *Seana-Chaint na dDéise* II, Dublin, 1961, 277.

23   In a Donegal Questionnaire reply.

24   See Ó Dónaill under *scréachóg*.

25   See Dineen under *gabhairín*.

26   See note 6 above.

27 Hall II, 1842, p. 106; [Mary E. Braddon] *Joshua Haggard's Daughter*, London 1876, 67; Jean Forbes, 'Folklore and Tradition in Glenvar, County Donegal', *Ulster Folklife* III, Part I (1957), 39.

28 IFC 26: 141.

29 These occur in questionnaire replies from Donegal, Galway and Tyrone. It is possible that the enquiry about the number of wails in question 7 in the Banshee Questionnaire (see note 4 above) has prompted answers which were not traditional in the respective areas.

30 C.W. von Sydow, *Selected Papers on Folklore*, Copenhagen 1948, 87.

31 IFCS 644: 104.

32 IFC 1840: 329, from County Westmeath.

33 Seán MacGiollarnáth, *Loinnir Mac Leabhair*, Dublin, 1936, 203.

34 *Éist* — be silent!, whist!, Ó Dónaill under *éist*.

35 For the effect on a dog of an encounter with a supernatural being, see Tomás de Bhaldraithe (eag.), *Seanchas Thomáis Laighléis*, Baile Átha Cliath 1977, 205.

36 For the power of horses to sense the presence of supernatural beings, see Dáithí Ó hÓgáin: 'An Capall i mBéaloideas na hÉireann', *Béaloideas* 45-7 (1977-9), 199-243.

Further reading

Patricia Lysaght, *The Banshee. A Study in Beliefs and Legends about the Irish Supernatural Death-Messenger*, Dublin, 1985.

Countess Markievicz, by Anna Nordgron, National Gallery of Ireland

The Historical Image

Margaret MacCurtain

The Irish literary imagination has, over centuries, stored certain images of women which exercise a powerful pull on the behaviour patterns of Irish society and resonate at many levels of Irish nationalism. Tracing these images back over the centuries, a 'type' of woman emerges, though the image has been shaped and remodelled by the changing *Zeitgeist*. W. B. Yeats evoked her as the *cailleach*, one of the stock figures of early Irish literature, whose age conceals her immortality.

Sometimes the etymology of a word is as significant as its literal meaning. *Caille*, denoting a veil, made its way into primitive Irish no later than the fifth century. It is not clear how it became assimilated into the word *cailleach* which from then onwards signified a 'nun' in the growing Christian society, while retaining in secular mythology its original meaning of 'old hag', and carrying with it overtones of the sacred. Thus in Frank O'Connor's 'The Old Woman of Beare' which he places in the ninth century, the old woman becomes a nun in a Christian community at the close of her long life as a goddess of love. Yeats, however, linked the image of the *cailleach*, or old hag, to that of the *spéirbhean*, the vision-woman dear to eighteenth-century Gaelic poets as a female image of captive Ireland seeking a male protector. With the dramatic presentation of his play *Cathleen Ni Houlihan* Yeats perpetuated into the twentieth century the femaleness of Ireland, linking with her destiny that of men ready to die to free her.

> *Peter:* Did you see an old woman going down the road?
> *Patrick:* I did not: but I saw a young girl, and she had the walk of a queen.

How far does the historical imagination deal with the subject of women in Irish history? What stores of memories are allowed to seep through into the upper layers of consciousness either at folk level, or into the accepted version of our past? Making visible hidden elements in the total experience of a country's history is largely a question of perception, a kind of intellectual consciousness-raising. It is rare for historical research to accomplish the task of getting a society to contemplate its own identity without the help of literature as an auxiliary. The clues to the position of women in Irish history are invariably present in the literature of a particular phase of Irish history.

The significance of the idea of the femaleness of Ireland has not escaped the attention of scholars of early Irish history and of Celtic mythology over the decades. 'It would be hard to exaggerate the importance of this idea of the land and its sovereignty conceived in the form of a woman,' remarks Proinsias Mac Cana in his study of women in Irish mythology.

> From the beginning of history and before, until the final dissolution of the Irish social order in the seventeenth century, traditional orthodox thought was dominated by this image of the *puella senilis*, the woman who is literally as old as the hills yet endlessly restored to youth through union with her rightful mate. She outlives not only men but also tribes and peoples.

Furthermore the goddess is the symbol of the land and only by uniting with her can the ruler become acceptable to his people, and she, joined with the rightful ruler, becomes young and beautiful once more. Mac Cana, turning to the historians, puts the question succinctly:

> ... it is nevertheless reasonable to ask whether a society which in its literature attributes such independence to its women characters as does much of early Irish literature would on the other hand deny it or rigidly curtail it in real life.[1]

Women in Early Irish Society

Even now it remains true that the history of women in Early Christian Ireland is largely unwritten. Though the sources are abundant, they remain scattered. In his contribution to *Women in Irish Society* Donncha Ó Corráin examined the position of women before the law in early Irish society. Women had extensive rights in marriage contracts, over property, in divorce and marital arrangements, and in their responsibility towards their children.[2] According to the earliest law-tracts it would seem that by the beginning of the eighth century women had progressed from a situation in which they had little independent legal power to one of equality with their husbands. A serious study is now required of that first period reconciling the discrepancies that suggest the presence of female power in the sagas set in the historical period of the seventh century, and in the hagiographical material surrounding the lives of female Celtic saints, notably Brigid, with the evidence of women's legal incapacity in the earliest of the law-tracts. Liam de Paor, in an unpublished paper which he delivered to the Dublin Historical Association in 1975, and D. A. Binchy, in his *Studies in Early Irish Law* (Royal Irish Academy 1936), buttress the conviction that early Irish society was patriarchal in the sense that politics and law were governed by men. Binchy suggests that the influence of the Christian Church may have helped to bring about the change noticeable in the eighth and ninth centuries. Yet another point of view is expressed by Eoin Mac Neill when he suggests that the women in early Irish society enjoyed a fairly decent status in literature and in life which may have derived from the customs and legal usages of pre-Celtic peoples which, over time, influenced the law-tracts of their conquerors.[3] Writing on the development of women's rights in in ninth and tenth centuries. Ó Corráin notes that the privileges of 'the woman of equal lordship' were by that time extended to the wives of a lower grade, thus extending it to the majority of married women. In general the property laws were equitable to women and men and the rights of children were safe-guarded by a legal designation of responsibility between fathers and mothers.

 ,litically, the woman who in literature is closely associated with the sovereignty myth did not inherit power, nor did she govern as an independent sovereign. Nevertheless there is similarity between Medb (Maeve) of the Táin Bó Cuailnge whose sexual indulgence conceals her primary function as a goddess of sovereignty, and the christianised Brigid, founder of the great monastery of Kildare which, under her rule and that of her successors as abbesses, laid claim to a wide parouchia of over thirty churches around AD 630. Though Brigid was under the authority of the Church as a consecrated nun, her jurisdiction over the local Church in Leinster was undisputed at a period when the organisation of the Irish Church was far from complete. Not only did she assume spiritual responsibility for the Christian people around the monastery that she founded in Kildare, but the seventh century *Life* by Cogitosus speaks of 'her See . . . episcopal and virginal', and the Book of Armagh invokes her: 'O Brigid, your parouchia within your own province will be reputed as your kingdom.' John Ryan remarks:

> This seems to suggest that the abbess of *Cill Dara* wielded 'monarchial' authority over all the churches and church lands attached to her monastery within the Kingdom of Leinster. It would appear, also, that with the approval of the primates of Armagh later abbesses of Kildare, if not St Brigid herself, exercised some kind of jurisdiction at Kildare and elsewhere . . . From the evidence there seems to be no doubt that Brigid's successors exercised some of the functions more generally restricted to bishops.[4]

Brigid's capabilities can be measured by the near contemporary testimonies to her skill as a chariot-driver, her ease in the company of men, and her achievements as the founder of a large double monastery where celibate men and women attended vast numbers of the sick and weary.

Brigid's Kildare was founded towards the close of the fifth century, and its rise coincided with a period of transition in the Irish Church in which a number of female Irish saints came to be important Christian leaders in their local communities. Saint Ite of Kileedy in County Limerick was a hermit of the heroic dimensions we associate with the Egyptian desert hermits: in her case she communed with God rather than wrestled with devils. Saint Moninne of Sliab Cuilinn (Killeevey) was the leader of her community on the borders of Louth—Armagh and was a friend and collaborator of Brigid's. Patrick, according to his biographer Tirechan, initiated his missionary policy by placing women in leadership roles whenever the occasion required it. A more detailed scrutiny is now required of the part played by women saints in the age of transition after Patrick and later in the *Celi Dé* movement under the influence of Samthann, abbess of Clonbroney (*c.* 730) in order to understand what they possessed in terms of prestige, power and authority — and how much was lost in the centuries following the decline of Celtic monasticism.

Women in the Viking and Norman Period

Ó Corráin detects a major rise in the political status of women by the middle of the tenth century, consorts or wives of kings then assuming the title of queen. History and propaganda are deeply intertwined in this middle period. Gormlaith, for instance, ex-consort of Brian Boru, persists in Irish folk-lore as a strong political woman of the eleventh century, and An tAthair Peadar O Laoghaire, in his historical saga *Niamh*, (*Celtica* 1907), revived for nationalist readers of the early years of the Gaelic League a story of the Viking period which, though simplistic and tedious, juxtaposes two women, one from the Viking world, Gormlaith, and the other, Niamh, from the Celtic world as imagined in the late nineteenth century. Gormlaith deserves to be reset in Irish history and rescued from the pro-Brian propagandists of the twelfth century. What is clear is that the position of high-born women in early Irish society was in comparatively high profile; wielding influence and power, they possessed a freedom before the law quite astonishing in comparison with the stunting imposition of feudal and later English law upon the position of women in society.

What women lost in Norman Ireland in the way of legal rights and freedoms in the areas of marriage and divorce was partially offset by their admittance into a larger European milieu. It was a high price to pay. The position of women in western Europe was diminished after the Crusades. Claude Levi-Strauss puts it pithily, reviewing the effect of Islam on the western world at the time of the Crusades: 'it was then that the west lost the opportunity of remaining female'. Whatever the reasons, Anglo-Norman Ireland, in its legal attitude to women, curtailed their freedom both as wives and daughters. The Anglo-Normans operated a system of customary law which was a reflection of prevailing feudal practices and was to become over centuries the corpus of English common law. Among the restrictive practices, it gave the husband complete control of his wife's property, and he became his wife's sole guardian. It gave parents the authority to arrange a marriage for their daughter without her consent. This was particularly poignant in the case of child-marriages, and the Church sought to ameliorate the harshness of secular law by insisting on the 'free will' clause when both parties came of age. The marriage of Aoife, daughter of the King of Leinster, to the Norman invader, Strongbow, has always been regarded as significant in the course of Irish history. In Norman law she became an heiress, thus allowing her husband to claim as her property the lordship of Leinster. In political terms, she was a captive princess handed over as part of the spoils of war, and the marriage marked a decisive change in the position of women in Norman Ireland. As Katharine Simms remarks: 'Anglo-Irish husbands might have masterful wives, but since in law they had no independent control of their property, the women had to exercise their influence indirectly by putting pressure on their menfolk.'[5] It was as a dowered widow with a life-interest in one-third or half of the property of her late husband that the Anglo-Norman woman enjoyed a measure of independence. But the Anglo-Norman world in the late middle ages in Ireland was one of hazardous exploitation for the heiress marrying into an Anglo-Norman lordship.

In contrast, in those parts of Ireland where Gaelic law and rule prevailed, the wife of the Irish ruler preserved financial control over her dowry, and was entitled to certain rents and taxes from her husband's subjects. Notably in the sixteenth century, the political power of the Irish woman administering either her husband's business while he was at war — as with Iníon Dubh, mother of Red Hugh O'Donnell, or her own estate, as in the case of Gráinne O'Malley — was an excercise of customary right, hallowed by tradition. She was expected to participate in council in times of war, to negotiate hostages, and even to determine succession to the throne. The sixteenth century is, *par excellence*, a century of Tudor women in Ireland. Queen Anne Boleyn, with her Irish background of Ormonde-Butler connections, was eclipsed by her vigorous daughter Queen Elizabeth I. She was matched by an unparalleled gallery of Irish women, challenging, haughty, toughly negotiating for their menfolk and for retention of their territory: Joan Butler Fitzgerald, the war-torn wives of the Maguires and the O'Donnells, Catherine Magennis, who accompanied the Earl Hugh O'Neill in his exile to Rome after 1603, and many more awaiting discovery. It was a great century for women in Irish history, and a terrible one in the aftermath of their eclipse. Living in genteel poverty on the continent as the wives and daughters of Wild Geese in the following century, we catch a glimpse of their indomitable spirit in the figure of Lady Rosa O'Doherty, the energetic wife of the military commander Eoghan Roe O'Neill.[6]

One other aspect of the position of these high-born ladies is to be noticed. The wider orbit of European influence associated with the Normans introduced into Ireland cultural themes which are brought together in the collection of poetry known as courtly love. As a literary *genre* this body of erotic poetry written in fourteenth- and fifteenth-century Irish has received due attention from Robin Flower in *The Irish*

Tradition (Oxford 1947) and subsequently in an outstanding work by Seán Ó Tuama, *An Grá in Amhráin na nDaoine* (Cork 1949). The same poetry which Flower and Ó Tuama scrutinise for the impact of the Provençal literary forms and style upon Irish poetry yields evidence of social attitudes in what was essentially an aristocratic expression crossing the boundaries of Anglo-Norman and Gaelic. In Ireland there was no Albigensian heresy to isolate the poet and his mistress. Rather there was a teasing pre-occupation with the external delights of the beloved. Female beauty is stereotyped in these poems much as Hollywood imprisoned the notional (as distinct from the ideal) in the mid-twentieth century. Some of the poets were women but they belonged to an aristocracy and took their part lightheartedly in the witty exchanges about the nature of jealous love:

> If he kill me through jealousy now
> His wife will perish of spite,
> *He'll* die of grief for his wife —
> Three of us dead in a night.
>
> ('A Learned Mistress' in Frank O'Connor,
> *Kings, Lords and Commons*)

In a different mood, the satire and 'praise' poems of sixteenth-century Ireland carry overtones of inclusion and exclusion, a whole world of approval of women by men, in this case the *filí* or poets, which still awaits an interpretation.

Women in Transition

Even a cursory glance at sixteenth-century Gaelic society suggests a female—male complementarity and some presence of female autonomy, as in the evidence of women participating in decision-making procedures; the marriage of older women to younger men; female support among in-laws (as in the Geraldine conspiracy of *c.* 1539); and the presence of women's quarters in the tower-houses. Subordination of women became a reality in the following centuries. With the destruction of the medieval Gaelic and Anglo-Norman institutions by the Elizabethan conquest, Ireland entered into a period of colonisation from which it did not emerge until the early twentieth century. In the seventeenth century plantations — the Plantation of Ulster (1609), the large-scale Cromwellian settlement in mid-century and the final phase at the end of the century — linked with a penal code of legislation connected the subduing of the native population to the particular subjugation of women.

The conquest and plantations of the sixteenth and seventeenth centuries transformed the political, social and economic structure of Irish society. From then until the great Famine of the mid-nineteenth century there are only three general statements which can with any confidence be made concerning the role of women in that society. Firstly, they were totally without formal political rights; secondly, their property and inheritance rights, both within and outside of marriage, were now governed by English common law; and thirdly, theirs was a subject and subsidiary role to the male, and it was performed, for the most part, within a domestic context.

Thus Gearóid Ó Tuathaigh begins his investigation of the role of women under what he terms 'the new English order'. Ó Tuathaigh's essay is concerned with the role of women in those centuries, mainly seventeenth and eighteenth, in the social and economic spheres, and he looks at the residual cultural differences between planter and Gael, and sees the role of women as above all else 'a function of class'.[7]

Implicit in his examination is the background of colonisation. Colonisation in seventeenth-century Ireland, while it differed in certain respects from that of the new world for historical reasons, bore the same general characteristics which have marked it everywhere, that of a stratified state won by military conquest. There was a growth in state bureaucracy as plantation and settlement by foreigners succeeded in utilising the country's resources in what amounted to a structural transformation of the older, pastoral economy. The consolidation of wealth in the hands of great landowners resulted in the emergence of an aristocracy whose power was buttressed by force and legislation. Throughout the seventeenth century there was the painful emergence of a minimally consuming class of producers who, by the beginning of the eighteenth century, can be discerned as the labouring poor at the bottom of a class pyramid whose upper layers of nobility, administrators, churchmen, army officers and great merchants appropriated their labour and produce.

Eighteenth-century Ireland remained a pre-industrial stratified society whose wealth was based on landownership and the management of great estates. The severity of the Penal Code (1691–1715) which stripped a subdued conquered population of the right to ownership was, in the case of Ireland, discriminatory on the grounds of religion. In particular the Roman Catholic and Presbyterian small leaseholders suffered. Those groups or individuals who could alleviate their exploitation tended to take advantage of the unjust system, and the emergence of farming and commercial interests in eighteenth-century Ireland, while it brought prosperity to some classes, did not bring about a collective resistance to colonial oppression. The spiral towards a rising population, particularly at the lower end of the social scale, quickened alarmingly in the last decades of the eighteenth century and hastened the disastrous Famine of 1846. Then a country which had tried to support eight million people faced the breakdown of a rural economy unable to cope with the numbers.

The effects of colonisation on women cannot be disassociated from the effects on society as a whole. English law was introduced from the beginning of the seventeenth century. All the Churches after the Reformation placed women in a subordinate position within the family and the patriarchal nuclear family became the ultimate model in colonial systems. In Ireland, women became virtual minors before the law, 'privatised' in their life-style, and admonished by the Churches to be obedient to their husbands.

Native Irish poetry reflected this quenching of womanly graces and spirit. In general the poets wrote bitter-sweet poetry about the decline of the old order, and in the memorable 'Cill Chais' (*c.* 1720) the unknown poet made reference to the lady of the great house now in ruins:

> Her company now must lament her,
> Who would give yellow money and white
> But who'd never take land from the people
> But was friend to the truly poor.
> (Translated by Thomas Kinsella in *An Duanaire*)

Within a generation the major poets were writing of the captive *spéirbhean* who was a figure of unliberated Ireland needing to be rescued by her 'prince' across the waters of Europe. Occasionally she was depicted in bondage to the powerful John Bull, who emerged as the symbol of England after the campaigns of Marlborough and in the early eighteenth century. The *aisling* or vision poetry of this period simultaneously projects for the listeners the ideal of the 'passive' beautiful young woman. If she appears supernatural as in Egan O'Rahilly's 'Brightness of Brightness', she does not possess the powers of the ninth-century hag of Beare. Those men who wrote *aisling* poetry spoke to a rural population, conveying through the poems feelings of helplessness, sorrow and pathos. The folk-songs of this period, however abundant and varied, reflect in many cases the passivity and powerlessness of the lovers.

In stark contrast to the powerlessness of the eighteenth-century *spéirbhean* as depicted in the *aisling* poetry, the lament for Art Ó Laoghaire composed by his wife, Eibhlin Dhubh Ní Chonaill, is a splendidly sustained work sparkling with anger and grief over the murder of her husband. Apart from its merit as a social and historical document, this fine poem has a distinction of form and theme and well deserves the honourable place it holds in Gaelic literature to the present day. It orchestrates all the wordless grief that the 'keening' women uttered over the bodies of the dead in rural Ireland, and its preservation in the oral tradition of the people of Cork and Kerry established it securely as one of the great laments and love poems in the Gaelic tongue.

> My love and my mate
>   That I never thought dead
> Till your horse came to me
>   With bridle trailing,

All blood from forehead
 To polished saddle
Where you should be
 Either sitting or standing,
I gave one leap to the threshold,
 A second to the gate,
A third upon its back,
 I clapped my hands,
And off at a gallop;
 I never lingered
Till I found you lying
 By a little furze-bush.
(From 'The Lament for Art O'Leary in Frank O'Connor,
Kings, Lords and Commons)

Irish women in the colonial world of eighteenth-century Ireland responded to their condition by establishing their own coping strategies. Recognition of being oppressed does not preclude recognition on the part of the oppressed that they are capable of acting to influence their own destiny. Young women began to emigrate to the new world, and later to Australia, first incidentally in the 1790s, and then in growing numbers in the early nineteenth century, and eventually in a steady stream throughout the following century to a world where they could hope to better themselves and their relatives. A study of Quaker women reveals their social awareness and activity right through this period. They were in the forefront for reform.

Among the Roman Catholic population, the most consistent expression of women prepared to defend the collective interests of their people was the rise of women's religious orders. In particular the native sisterhoods, such as the Presentation Sisters founded by Nano Nagle for the education of poor children, the Irish Sisters of Loreto founded by Mary Ward to provide home-based schooling for the daughters of the rising middle classes, and the Sisters of Mercy founded by Catherine McAuley, devoted to the alleviation of human suffering and misery wherever they found it, became the clamant voice of the oppressed.

As for the women of the ascendancy in eighteenth-century Ireland, they too emerged from the shadows cast by the class-pyramid and made their contribution in places like Carton House and its rival Castletown House. Emily, Duchess of Leinster, though an Englishwoman by birth, ranks with those Irish women who understood the currents of freedom that were awakening in the colonies of North America and Ireland in the 1770s. She was the mother of Lord Edward Fitzgerald, and had given him a liberal education which he was later to use in imbibing the ideas of the French Revolution; he joined the United Irishmen in 1796 and was fatally wounded a year later while evading arrest. His aunt, Lady Louise Connolly of Castletown, made heroic efforts to reach him before he expired. The ladies of Ireland's great demesnes, though they came from different traditions and of non-native stock, identified with the landscape and possessed an affinity with the Butler gentlewomen who presided over Cill Chais. The aristocracy feature in the fiction of Maria Edgeworth, and Yeats describes the women of a later gentry:

> The light of evening, Lissadell,
> Great windows open to the south,
>   Two girls in silk kimonos both
> Beautiful, one a gazelle.

Into Modern Times

The experience of women throughout the nineteenth century was one of gradual awakening, first to their condition, and their economic plight, and then hesitantly to their educational and legal rights. In 1825 there appeared a work of over two hundred pages from the pen of Cork-born William Thompson, *An Appeal of One Half of the Human Race, WOMEN, Against the Pretensions of the Other Half, MEN, to Retain Them in Political and Thence in Civil and Domestic Slavery*. This well-written and impassioned tract was probably inspired by the situation of Thompson's friend, the spirited Anna Wheeler, god-daughter of Henry Grattan, who endured twelve years of matrimonial misery in Limerick before gaining her liberation in London and becoming a remarkable personality, urging on Daniel O'Connell and his circle the notion of women's equality with men. Thompson's work deserves to be remembered: it was a sharp rebuttal of James Mill's argument in his 'Essay on Government' that women did not need formal political rights as they were adequately represented by their menfolk. Thompson reduced Mill's specious logic to absurdity and presented the argument of political rights for women so cogently that it exerted a strong influence on Daniel O'Connell who frequently asserted that the equality of women was irrefutable.[8] Both men cited Mary Wollstonecraft as one of their mentors.

Mill's son, John Stuart Mill, made amends for his father's austere views on women in his own famous essay 'The Subjection of Women'. John Stuart Mill also presented the first women's suffrage petition to the British House of Commons. That petition was signed on behalf of Irish Women by Anna Haslam from Youghal. Of Quaker stock she, with her husband Thomas, formed the first Suffrage Society in Ireland. In turn they influenced Hanna Sheehy and her husband, Owen Skeffington, who, with a group of women and men, brought political equality a step further by their agitation about the Vote For Women issue with the Home Rule Party from 1910 onwards. Simultaneously James Connolly and the Larkins concerned themselves with the economic rights of Irish women workers overtaken by the severity of factory conditions in Belfast and Dublin, and by the general oppression of poverty and servile work.

There was then a broad current of liberal thought about the emancipation of women flowing into the revolutionary atmosphere of the early twentieth century. Many factors contributed to its vigour, most notably the education of middle-class women in Ireland from the 1830s onward. With the securing of Catholic Emancipation, convent boarding schools for Catholic girls sprang up all over Ireland: the Ursuline, Loreto, Dominican and Sacré Coeur orders all established schools which survive into the late twentieth century. In the older schools founded in the 1830s and 1840s cultural and moral instruction was accompanied by the teaching of music, needlework, art and elocution in a curriculum that was not part of the State system. The task of turning young girls into young ladies was effectively accomplished through the teaching of Christian values and social aptitudes. The founding of Alexandra College in 1866 for the 'higher education of girls' marked a distinct step forward in the aspirations not only of the Protestant girls for whom it generally catered, but also for Catholic girls who aspired to university education. The establishment of the Dominican College for girls at Eccles Street and Loreto Abbey in Rathfarnham, in particular, sharpened the perceptions of girls' education at a time when the late 1870s threw public examinations open to girls and women. For the first time, girls' schools in Ireland could participate in public examinations and avail of entry into careers and professions. The effect of the 1878 Intermediate Act on Irish women cannot be over-estimated. It achieved a major revolution in their economic and educational aspirations which brought Irish women in the late nineteenth and early twentieth centuries under the spell of the liberalising influences of the feminist movement in America and Britain. Thus it was that higher education for middle-class Irish women brought them not only economic freedom and university honours, but in the early twentieth century brought them, by various routes, into the revolutionary experience that led to the founding of the Free State in the south in 1922.

James Connolly's words on the conditions of the working-class woman in the early twentieth century were also valid for much of the previous century:

> Driven out to work at the earliest possible age, she remains fettered to her wage-earning, a slave all her life. Marriage does not mean for her a rest from outside labour . . . she has added the duty of a double domestic toil — completing each day's work, she becomes the slave of domestic needs of family.

The rising aspirations of Irish society, observable by the second decade of the nineteenth century, did not continue to be favourable to the condition of working women, whether on farms or in the cities and towns. The catastrophe of the Famine (1846-47) had far-reaching effects on women, some of which escape historical research.[9] J. J. Lee puts the historical phenomenon succinctly when he observes: 'The great Famine drastically weakened the position of women in Irish society . . . economic circumstances therefore conspired to make Ireland an increasingly male dominated society after the Famine.'[10]

The falling status of women and the predicament of the unmarried daughter in rural Ireland had its counterpart in the urban centres. Though status in post-Famine Ireland was not determined by gender, the emergence of single women as a large group — 43.3 per cent of the total female population in 1861 — is in itself a significant commentary.[11] Within that substantial group — by 1911 it was up to 48.6 per cent — there were class groupings with structurally differential access to resources and even subsistence. It is possible to differentiate between rural and urban women and to make distinctions between the working-class woman and the middle- and upper-middle class woman, but the overall choice of women was between being married and by law the property of their husbands and remaining single and in a vulnerable economic and social role, whether on the farm or factory floor.

The majority of Irish women were left largely unaffected by the early industrial revolution and the loss of status experienced by Irish women throughout the century was matched by their diminishing representation in the work-force. The same census of 1861 recorded 29 per cent of women employed. By 1911 only 19.5 per cent of women were employed. Mary E. Daly, in a wide-ranging paper delivered to the Irish Labour History First International Conference, noted that trends in women's employment have never paralleled their role in Irish society. Undoubtedly there was under-representation of women in the recording of the work-force, in the farm household and even in dressmaking. She concluded:

> . . . the typical working woman was either a domestic servant, a low grade textile or dress-making worker, or an agricultural labourer. Such women worked, not as a means of self-fulfillment, but simply because they had no real alternative.

The centrality of women to the Irish revolution of 1916—21 can be interpreted in a number of ways. Mainly their participation is seen as that of women engaging in a war of liberation with their menfolk. The role played by Cumann na mBan, the para-military organisation which was founded in the wake of the Irish Volunteers, still awaits a historian. The presence of a woman, Countess Markiewicz, in the 1916 Rebellion and her assumption of command of one of the fighting positions in Dublin city has been repeated in subsequent wars of liberation of this twentieth century. Perhaps it required a poet to kindle the imagination of an apathetic people; the sensitivity of W. B. Yeats in catching the resonances of the female presence in the events of the historic years of the Irish revolution was atavistic in its reminder of a Celtic past. More insistent for the historian now is the theme of women's resistance to colonisation, which finds its form in action that represented a struggle against oppression instead of an accommodation to it. As such, the participation of women in the revolutionary movement in Ireland can be seen as a fore-

runner of the unified action of women and men in Third World revolutionary movements of the twentieth century.

What then was the reality for the Irish woman in the decade following
Yeats's romantic projection of her female presence in Irish nationalism?
The participation of women in the national struggle was a short-lived
phenomenon. Overtaken by the forces of counter-revolution (again, a
familiar pattern in Third World revolutionary uprisings in the twentieth
century) Irish women retreated into a secondary role with the setting up
of the northern State in 1920 and the Free State in the south in 1922.
Around Irish women, as in a cage, were set the structures of family life
and women were assigned a home-based, full-time role as housewives,
whose talents and energies were devoted to looking after husband and
children.

Historians have tended to explain the illiberal legislation and stifling
provincialism of the post-Civil War decades in the Irish Free State by
referring to the value system of a tradition-minded, rural-orientated
society. Rarely, if at all, is allusion made to the total exclusion of woman
from public life, and from responsibility for public morality. Woman's
place was in the home. The sanctity of the marriage bond and the in-
dissolubility of marriage were upheld, civil divorce being ruled out by a
Dáil motion of 1925. The Juries Act of 1927 virtually excluded women
from jury service. Legislation on aspects of censorship was passed: in
1923 films 'subversive of public morality' were cut and refused a licence
by a male censor; six years later the Censorship of Publications Act em-
powered a board of five men to prohibit the sale of any book or period-
ical it considered 'indecent or obscene' or 'advocating the unnatural pre-
vention of conception'. In 1935 the sale, advertising or importation of
contraceptives was prohibited by Section 17 of the Criminal Law
(Amendment) Act. In 1927 the Catholic hierarchy had issued a joint
pastoral entitled 'The Evils of Modern Dancing' which deplored the
destruction of 'the characteristic virtues of our race', and listed the
dance-hall, the bad book, the film and immodest fashions in female dress
as contributing to the general decline of public morals. The Public Dance
Halls Act 1935 gave discretionary powers to District Justices to restrict
and regulate local dances. In 1937 the new constitution declared in
Article 41.2: 'In particular, the State recognises that by her life within
the home, woman gives to the State a support without which the
common good cannot be achieved.'

A deep perplexity about their true identity as citizens was felt by
many women. The anomaly of married women being constrained not to
work by State policy was compounded by the extension of State responsibilities for the provision of health and child-care services into the home,
thus ultimately diminishing her status. Nor is it fanciful to read into
Brian Merriman's great poem, 'The Midnight Court', written in Irish at the
end of the eighteenth century and translated by Frank O'Connor in the
twentieth century (and promptly banned by the Censorship Board) a
sense of the poet's dismay at the lack of harmony between the sexes:

colonisation always creates antagonism between men and women, and in such a situation their interests do not always coincide.

On a wider canvas it seems probable that the twentieth century will be seen as the century of the 'feminine mystique' in the context of women's history. All the major problems for women appear at one time or another, such as their questioning of war, their economic independence and their psychological liberation. The issue of birth control is one of profound interest to the Irish woman from the Famine onwards, but it was to remain an unresolved area of Irish family life. The majority of Irish women north and south view the two decades after 1921 as crucial to their experience of being female in Ireland. Self-determination was to come tardily, but it was to come surprisingly to the older woman as well as to the young, to the widow as well as to the married woman, to the woman in paid employment as well as to the woman working at home. And the debate was to be about equality of opportunity.

Notes

1   P. MacCana, 'Women in Irish Mythology', *The Crane Bag* 4, 1 (1980), p.7.
2   D. Ó Corráin, 'Women in Early Irish Society', *Women in Irish Society* (ed. MacCurtain, Ó Corráin), Dublin, 1978, pp 1-13.
3   E. MacNeill, *Early Irish Laws and Institutions*, London, 1935, pp 64-6.
4   J. Ryan, S.J., *Saint Brigid of Cill Dara*, Dublin, 1978, pp 8, 9.
5   K. Simms, 'Women in Norman Ireland' in *Women in Irish Society*, pp 14-25.
6   J. Causway, 'Lady Rosa O'Doherty' to be published in *Women in the Irish Tradition* (forthcoming).
7   G. Ó Tuathaigh, 'The Role of Women in Ireland under the New English Order' in *Women in Irish Society*, pp 26-36.
8   Professor M. O'Connell editor of *The O'Connell Letters* (I.M.C.), has kindly drawn my attention to this aspect of Daniel O'Connell's relationship with his wife.
9   The incidence of depression among categories of Irish women is currently being researched and links with emigration of whole households of children from maternal roof is a case in point.
10   J.J. Lee, 'Women in the Church since the Famine' in *Women in Irish Society*, pp 41-2.
11   M.B. Daly, 'Women in the Irish Workforce from pre-industrial to modern times' in *Saothar* 7 (1982), pp 74-81.

Women in Ulster

Miriam Daly

The history and social role of Irish woman is a new field for inquiry.[1]
The liberation of women is the most profoundly revolutionary task
civilised society can tackle. This task is fundamentally revolutionary
because relations between men and women are embedded in almost every
social relationship and institution. Sylvia Meehan, Chairperson of the
Employment Equality Agency which was set up by Dáil Eireann to
monitor and advise on the Equal Pay Legislation of 1974 and 1977,
expressed this very well in her paper which was read at a seminar in
Dublin in November 1978 on 'Women's Place in the Irish Economy,
Present and Future':

> Human nature will readily acknowledge the interdependence of
> work and family, production and reproduction, but human
> memories are so short that we need to be reminded that this inter-
> dependence got a new twist when industrialisation separated work
> places from homes and supported an ideology which ascribed to
> women the primary responsibility for providing domestic services
> for all other members of the family, including the young, the old
> and the sick. This ideology affects all women, whose availability
> and commitment is taken for granted. So much so that instead of
> being rewarded they are penalised. It encompasses those women
> who are not and never have been mothers, it exploits all women . . .
> Greater division of labour in the family and the workplace has
> affected the character of both and produced situations of divided
> loyalties and conflicting values.

A conviction of the totality of the human experience of life, of the
unity of the goals of liberation, of the inseparability of the individual's
public and private worlds, of the impossibility of woman's liberation in
an environment of economic or political repression, underlies the
approach taken to the struggle for the liberation of Ulster women in this
essay, as it pervades the thinking of Irish women who have been in the
leadership of the struggle for women's liberation, from Anna Wheeler to
Louie Bennett, first woman President of the Irish Congress of Trade
Unions in 1933, to Bernadette Devlin McAliskey, youngest ever popularly
elected MP when she was returned in 1969.

An important factor in shaping the role of Ulster women was their industrial environment. Ireland's major manufacture, linen, was carried on in Ulster on a domestic basis after 1660. It became increasingly important to the economy up to the outbreak of the Revolutionary and Napoleonic Wars in 1793.

In the enforced peace which followed the Cromwellian conquest, Ulster was regarded as the poorest of the provinces. An indicator of this is the relative amounts of land offered to persons who lent money to pay the English army under the terms of the Adventurers' Act 1642. One acre of land was to be granted in Ulster for every four shillings advanced, one acre of Connacht land for every six shillings, one acre of Munster land for every twelve shillings, and one acre of County Dublin land for every pound sterling. These values could not have reflected the relative productive capacity of the land but reflect rather contemporaries' views of the relative desirability of residence in the respective provinces and their assessment of the law and order situation.

When the peace of conquest came the people returned to their old settlements or made new ones. The Protestants were in the valleys and on the good land; the Catholics retreated to the hills and bogs, such as the highlands of Donegal, which to the present constitute the most vigorously Irish-speaking and Gaelic of the Irish Gaeltacht areas.

Ulster thrived and prospered and the linen manufacture of cloth produced on the domestic system from largely home-grown flax was at the heart of this prosperity. Spinning and weaving were carried on in the home in a pre-industrial process. Women and children, old and young, worked indoors or in the fields in a continuous round of activity. The household was the unit of production and in its operation and management the mother was an essential and equal partner, though the weaving process and attending markets were regarded as the man's spheres. There was complete unity between public and private roles. Work and leisure were not separated, and on feast-days or days of funerals the whole household took time off. Woman was not oppressed within the household, though she shared the oppression experienced by her class. The additional earnings provided by the sale of the webs of cloth led to relative prosperity. Gaiety abounded, there was great interest in clothes and amusements, the people were self-confident and the wife rode pillion behind her husband to chapel or church or meeting on Sundays.

A poem by Thomas Beggs reflects the contrast between domestic work and the lot of women working in factories. It is called 'The Auld Wife's Address to her Spinning Wheel'. Two verses are quoted to illustrate this point:

> Frae Tibbie Gordon I gat this wheel,
> An' then I was young an' my face was fair
> An' since the first day she cam' into my shiel,
> We aye had something to keep and to spare.
> On the wintry night by the clear ingle side,

My wee bit lamp hung high in the lum,
An' I sang my song, an' my wheel I plied,
An' Rorie was pleased wi' the heartsome hum.
But now upon her I maun spin nae mair,
An' it makes my heart baith sorry an' sair.

The mountain lass at her wee bit wheel,
How blythe was her e'e an' how rosy her cheek;
Her bosom was white, an' her heart was leal,
Her mien it was modest, her manner was meek;
But now the pert maidens, wha ply in the mill,
How wan is their visage, how dim is their e'e,
For the ban they maun bide is enough to chill
The spring of the heart an' to deaden their glee:
To toil for men that are hard to please
In a hot-bed rank wi' vice an' disease.

The fear of the moral corruption of factory workshops expressed in the last two lines is stated more bluntly by a correspondent to the *Belfast Newsletter* who wrote 'Live morality, perish factories'. The conservatism that was to become such a marked feature of Ulster Unionism and the distaste for public levity were already apparent in some elements of Ulster pre-Famine society. A different view of factories is expressed by the following anonymous ballad from Armagh town which praises a spinning mill.

Mr Jacob Orr's Spinning Mill

As I silently lay by a large flowing stream
A youth and a maiden did rove by the same,
He asked her the cause of such noise o'er the hill,
And she answered it's the music from Mr Orr's Mill.

Behold yon fine object appears in the air
You'll find great industry is carried on there;
My master has agents his orders to fill,
Mr Henry, young Wright, and the Clerk of the Mill

And hundreds beside me who would have been poor,
And forced out to wander from door unto door;
Were it not for the coin which is cast by his Mill,
And marked with the beautiful stamp, Laurelhill.

I have only quoted three of the ten stanzas of this ballad but it must have been inspired or printed by sources close to the management, as it is impossible to believe that any member of the Ulster working class at that time would have welcomed payment in token money. However, the evidence in Betty Messenger's book *Picking Up the Linen Threads* indicates that women had a light-hearted approach to work.

The mechanisation of the spinning process of linen manufacture led to the deepening of capitalism and the extension of the putting out process. The labour force in weaving was expanded to keep up with the output of cheap yarn whilst household earnings of the domestic workers were eroded by the reduction in earnings for the domestic spinning of home-grown flax. Women and young boys and girls were employed away from home as weavers. In County Down children of non-weaving parents were sent to weavers who taught them the trade in return for food, lodging and the agreement to stay with them for two or three years. Higher rates were paid for weaving in factories than could be earned domestically. As happened at Lowell in Massachusetts, a large weaving labour force divorced from the land was concentrated in the towns of County Down and in Belfast. They were mainly between fourteen and twenty years old, boys and girls, and they lived in houses provided by the employers, working long hours. In times of high food prices, as during the Great Famine, there were cases of families working around the clock on the loom, men and women, to earn the price of food (Handloom Weavers Committee, 1838). The possibility of such earnings did, however, lessen the number of deaths from hunger in Ulster during the Great Famine.

The mechanisation of the weaving process of linen manufacture was completed during the 1860s, and this brought the domestic system to an end. The location of the industry shifted east, and Belfast became the dominant centre. During the nineteenth century Belfast grew from a town of some 20,000 inhabitants in 1801 to one of over 350,000 in 1901, a rate of growth that was exceeded only by the fastest growing American cities. The numbers of small-holdings declined dramatically and the Ulster working class became increasingly a proletariat divorced from ownership or access to the means of production except on the strict terms dictated by their employers. Hiring fairs where young women sold their labour as farm servants for a season became common throughout the north. Young Donegal girls walked long distances to these fairs, where they were hired for work on the richer, larger farms on the eastern side of the province. Emigration was preferable if the means to emigrate were to hand.

In the second half of the nineteenth century the conditions of women in factories were oppressive. Wages were low, hours long, health poor, life-expectancy short, pregnancies frequent and infant mortality rates high. But because of the long history of manufacture in Ulster, and increased employment in the making-up trades — for example the shirt industry in Derry and the surrounding countryside, or the sprigging industry in Belfast and its hinterland — Ulster women had work opportunities apart from domestic service, which was the only opening for poor women in other provinces. This led to a militant determination which has become the hallmark of Belfast women in particular; and Belfast was where the majority of the province's working women lived by the end of the nineteenth century.

The growing dominance of Belfast was well expressed by J. W. Good, who wrote, in *Ulster and Ireland* (1919): 'Belfast is to Ulster what Paris is supposed to be to France. It imposes its will on the community and no movement succeeds to which it denies support . . . The combativeness of Belfast is equalled only by its self-assertiveness.'

The conditions in the factory were harsh. A striking woman factory worker told James Connolly in Belfast:

> . . . it's over forty-five years since I started work in the mills. I was just turned eight when I began. When you were eight you were old enough to work. Worked in steam, making your rags all wet, and sometimes up to your ankles in water. The older you got the more work you got. If you got married you kept on working. Your man didn't get enough for a family. You worked till your baby came, and went back as soon as you could, and then, God forgive you, you counted the years till your child could be a half-timer and started the same hell of a life again.

Messenger's work underlines the prevalence of child labour in the mills.[2]

Though the woman was a full, sometimes the sole, wage-earner, no special arrangements were made to help her with domestic work or in bringing up the children. James Connolly wrote about this in *The Re-Conquest of Ireland*:

> Driven out to work at the earliest possible age, she remains fettered to her wage-earning, a slave for life. Marriage does not mean for her a rest from outside labour, it usually means that to outside labour she has added the duty of double domestic toil . . . The worker is the slave of capitalist society, the female worker is a slave of that slave. In Ireland that female worker has exhibited in her martyrdom an almost damnable patience.

Whilst the majority of working-class women were becoming more oppressed, new opportunities were opening for women of the middle class and petty bourgeois families. Most of these were provided by the Churches and all were tinged by the spirit of Evangelicalism which became dominant after the sweeping success of the Great Revival movement of 1859, which became known in Ulster history as 'The Year of Grace'. On the Roman Catholic side, orders of nuns opened schools, hospitals, orphanages and homes for the physically and mentally handicapped all over Ulster. These gave opportunities to energetic women who were dedicated to the religious life to develop their gifts for administration and to serve wide sections of the community. Protestant women heard the call of foreign mission fields and their energy in evangelising in all the continents has yet to be chronicled. For example as early as the 1840s Ulster women were active in the missions to China. Philanthropy was the main outlet for the energies of the middle-class women who were totally freed from domestic work by the abundance and low wages of domestic servants.

The only way open to women working in manufactures to improve their conditions was through organisation in trade unions. Recent research has shown that women were involved in all the labour movements and trade agitations in Britain in the first half of the nineteenth century. There is every reason to assume that *a fortiori* they were even more heavily involved in Ireland, where women were frequently accepted as the tenant of the farm or small-holding and had to manage all the production when the husbands were away spalpeening (on migratory work). There is no evidence to indicate that agrarian agitations or factions were male-dominated. J. R. Fox's work on tenure and kinship on Tory Island shows that women inherited land and that the family was not patrilinear. The first major industrial conflicts in which women were involved on a large scale in Belfast were the linen strikes of 1872 and 1874. These were sparked off by strikes by the male flax dressers for increases in wages. The employers locked out all the workers, including the women and girls who comprised about 70 per cent of the work-force in the industry. They then tried to entice the women to return to work leaving the men locked out. Editorials in the *Newsletter* read: 'The women and the girls are blameless . . . They did not strike but because of the strike they were locked out and now they may get bread whatever way they please.'

The speeches which two women made at this time show their militancy and determination to resist attempts to divide them from the male workers:

> *Miss Brown:* Sisters, I believe we are all united here to stand as firm as a rock, and I hope, as I am informed that the gates are to be thrown open on Monday, that not one of us will be seen there, unless they put up a notice to give us our old wages . . . The profits of the mill owner are too great.
> *Miss Havelock:* . . . the masters have been raised from the dung pit to the hill. The workers have built them country sites, have shovelled money into them and there they stood without a friend . . . Oh ye poor oppressed sons and daughters of Erin: there is no country so oppressed. It is work or want.[3]

The organisation of women workers in the linen industry was not systematically undertaken, however, until the 1890s when visitors from the Women's Trade Union Provident League in England came to Belfast. Encouragement was given by the Belfast Trades Council, and an activist, Mary Galway, emerged, who became secretary of the first trade union for female textile workers in Ireland: the Textile Operatives' Society. In 1897 she led 8,000 workers in a strike against the enforcement of strict discipline and penalties in the factories and workshops under the provisions of the Truck Act (1896):

> Posting up a list of all rules and regulations as to fines and penalties which they (the employers) wished to enforce in their factories was accompanied by considerable agitation by the operatives in a large number of factories in Belfast and District refusing to work under the conditions formulated. The stoppage of work involving about 8,000 operatives began on January 19th. Negotiations between the Belfast Trades Council (in the person of Mary Galway) and the employers resulted in a provisional return to work on January 25th; the matter in dispute being left for settlement by subsequent negotiations. These resulted in considerable modifications of the rules originally posted.
>
> (P. P. Board of Trade, Report on Strikes and Lockouts 1898)[4]

This is the first instance in Ireland of a woman negotiating directly with the employers in a major trade dispute. These instances also show that despite what the literature constantly describes as the notorious difficulty of organising women workers, the Belfast linen operatives were as progressive politically as the cotton spinners in the north-west of England.

Mary Galway enjoyed the support of William Walker and other Belfast socialists in her organisational work, but like them she tended to concentrate her efforts on the better-paid Protestant workers and to be an economist in her approach to Irish workers' problems. By this I mean that agitation or discussion of the Irish national question was regarded as a diversion from more relevant preoccupations with immediate issues which were of interest to all members of the working class such as rates of wages or conditions of work. This group tried to prevent the affiliation of the Irish Transport and General Workers' Union to the Belfast Trades Council in 1907 and of the Irish Women Workers' Union and the Irish Textile Workers' Union which was a women's union organised by James Connolly amongst the most needy section of the mill girls who were untouched by Mary Galway's organisation.

Connolly came to Belfast as organiser of the Irish Transport and General Workers' Union in 1910 and lived with his family on the Falls Road. When new rules were introduced by the employers to tighten discipline in the factories and workshops the women again struck as in 1897 and they turned to James Connolly for leadership. Notices were posted throughout the workshops announcing a system of fines for, among other things, singing, laughing, talking, or 'adjusting the hair' during working hours. A girl who brought sweets or knitting needles into the mill could be instantly sacked. At a mass meeting held at St Mary's Hall in the centre of the city the girls unanimously passed a resolution condemning 'as a disgrace to civilisation the conditions sought to be imposed on us by the mill owners.' Connolly described the tactic he used to defeat the inhumanity of the employers:

I've advised them not to go back in ones and twos but to gather outside the mill and all go in as a body; to go in singing. If when at work one girl laughs and is reprimanded, they are all to begin laughing and if one girl sings and is checked, they are all to sing. And if a girl is dismissed for breaking the rules they are all to walk out with her. They have accepted the idea enthusiastically and before they left tonight they were busy making up a song to sing as they go back.

The employers gave up and the Belfast women workers had assured for themselves conditions of work which allowed some humanity and gaiety at their work.

Mary Galway resented Connolly's intrusion as organiser of women workers which she regarded as her sphere: 'Mr Connolly should confine himself to the operations of his own union and not trespass on the domain of a society that fought and was fighting the women's battle all along,' she commented. But other prominent women trade unionists emerged in Ulster.

The women's movement there took the same course as in the rest of Ireland, that is, there was growing awareness on the part of feminist activists of the unity of the women's, the economic and the national questions. For example, Marie Johnson, the wife of Tom Johnson, was the first unpaid secretary of the Irish Textile Workers' Union and also active in the Belfast Co-operative Society and the Irish Labour Party which her husband led in Dáil Eireann. Winnie Carney who first became involved in politics as a suffragist followed Connolly to Dublin, became his secretary and was the last woman to leave the GPO in 1916. Nelly Gordon who started life as a shawlie in the mills took a job as a full-time trade union official; she thereby suffered a reduction of wages from seventeen shillings and ninepence a week to seven shillings and sixpence.

It would be wrong to think that the tradition of activism amongst Ulster working-class women was confined to Belfast. When the Congress of the Irish Transport and General Workers' Union, by far the largest of the Irish trade unions, voted for a resolution in favour of equal pay for equal work in 1948 the case for women's rights was put by three Derry women: Margaret O'Donnell, Eileen Flynn and Doris Vorran. This was an important milestone on the way to the historic concession by the Dublin government on equal pay in 1975. But even during the years of retrenchment that followed on the Civil War, women trade unionists both North and South had broader preoccupations than purely women's rights. As Sylvia Meehan has expressed it:

Women's contribution has been a more generous one. They could have argued simply for equal pay and women's rights. They did more than this, bringing with them a humane concern for all of society's underprivileged and handicapped sections.

Notes

1 *Women in Irish Society, the Historical Dimension* edited by Margaret Mac-Curtain and Donncha Ó Corráin, Arlen House 1979 is the only work of any substance on the subject and it is required reading for all serious students of this question, as is Francis Devine's paper in *Obair* 2.
2 Betty Messenger, *Picking Up the Linen Threads*, Belfast 1981.
3 I owe these to Emily Boyle. (See her article, 'The Linen Strike of 1872', in *Saothar* 2, 1976).
4 Quoted in a paper read to the Women's Advisory Committee of the Irish Congress of Trade Unions by Francis Devine (1977).

Note on Miriam Daly

Miriam Daly was born on 16 May 1928 in the Curragh Camp in Kildare where her father Daniel McDonnell, a colonel in the Irish Army, was stationed. Her mother, Anne Cummins, was from a nearby farming family. Her father, who came from the Dublin working class and held strong labour views, had been on active service with Michael Collins in the Irish War of Independence. His father had been interned by the British in the same Ballykinlar military camp near Downpatrick where internees were held in 1971. Miriam graduated in economics and history from University College Dublin in 1948 and graduated MA with a thesis on Irish labour in England under the supervision of Professor George O'Brien. She was a lecturer in the Department of History at UCD from 1950 to 1953. In that year she married Dr Joseph Lee, who shared her searching, creative and generous approach to life.

She was an extra-mural history lecturer until 1958 when they moved to England, where Dr Lee was practising psychiatric medicine before his untimely death in 1963. Miriam continued to teach history and undertook research into agrarian distress and popular resistance in early nineteenth-century Ireland. In 1964 she became a lecturer in economic history at the University of Southampton. In 1965 she married James Daly, and in 1968 they returned to Ireland, where they took up posts in the departments of Scholastic Philosophy and Social and Economic History at Queen's University Belfast, where Miriam lectured until her death in 1980. In 1970 she and James adopted their twin children Marie and Donal. Soon after arrival in Belfast Miriam became involved with the Civil Rights movement, which soon ran up against brutal repression.

Miriam Daly always identified totally with the oppressed, and in the next few years she became an inspiring public speaker and an intrepid and indefatigable organiser. She joined the committee of the Northern Ireland Civil Rights Association in 1971 when the British and Stormont

(Northern Ireland) governments introduced internment without trial. After the Bloody Sunday outrages in 1972, she became dedicated to helping unite opposition North and South in Ireland to continued British and Unionist rule, which as she pointed out could no longer be imposed without naked terror and coercive rule.

As an economic historian, she also opposed the dishonest economism which diverted attention not only from political oppression (under the guise of demythologising and deromanticising Irish history) but also from the connection between political and social and economic structures. She was as aware as anyone of the subtleties and complexities of Irish as of all history, but, unfashionably, she did not allow that to distract her from the glaring structural realities. Miriam Daly's political and academic personality was integrated in a blazing sincerity which took her inside the Long Kesh compounds to lecture on her view of Irish history and her vision of an Irish future not only to Republican but to Loyalist prisoners, from whom she received personal messages of appreciation, and with whom she co-operated on welfare work. Her personal life was placed at the disposal of those who — temporarily — were greater victims of oppression than herself: the bereaved and prisoners and their families, who found her an unlimited well of spontaneous affection and vigorous support. It was a measure of her extraordinary energy that during this time she was also a founder member of the Economic and Social History Society of Ireland and of the Irish Labour History Society (and co-editor of *Saothar*). She was a frequent contributor to the Thomas Davis Lectures (two of her lectures are still to be published), *Philosophical Studies, Christus Rex, The Newman Review, History, Business History, Irish Economic and Social History, Ulster Folk Life.* At the time of her death she was working on a textbook of Irish economic history; in April of that year she was a delegate to the UNESCO Conference in Paris on labour history; for the commemorative volume for Professor Kenneth Connell she was preparing an article based on her work on agrarian agitation in nineteenth-century Munster; and she was about to revise greatly the article in this book which in its unfinished form has been edited for this collection. Her work and struggle for genuinely humane political and intellectual progress were cut short by her assassination in her home in Belfast on 26 June 1980.

Margaret MacCurtain

Changing Times for Women's Rights

Yvonne Scannell

The term 'women's rights' in this article has three different senses. Firstly, it refers to women's rights to be treated equally with men. Secondly, the term is used to refer to women's rights to be treated unequally from men — in other words, women's rights to be favoured or protected by the law. Finally, women's rights can refer to rights common to all Irish citizens but which affect women in a peculiar way and which only or substantially affect women for sociological, historical or biological reasons. Thus issues like contraception and the right to the communal ownership of family property are treated as women's issues because they affect women to a much greater extent than men.

The Irish constitution contains no less than six articles which, if boldly and imaginatively interpreted, could be read as vindicating the principle that women and men have equal rights. Article 9.1.3, which deals with nationality and citizenship, provides that 'No citizen may be excluded from Irish nationality and citizenship by reason of the sex of such person'. Article 16.1.2 provides that the right to vote resides in 'every citizen without distinction of sex'. Article 40.1 guarantees that 'All citizens shall, as human persons, be held equal before the law', though it recognises the inevitability, and thus the legitimacy, of legislative classifications by going on to provide that the guarantee of equality does not mean that 'the State shall not in its enactments have due regard to differences of capacity, physical and moral, and of social function'.

In Article 40.2.3 the State guarantees in its laws 'to respect and, so far as practicable, by its laws to defend and vindicate the personal rights of the citizen' (which term includes the female citizen) and to 'defend from unjust attack and, in the case of injustice done, vindicate the life, person, good name and property rights of every citizen'. Article 41.2 recognises, long before the Irish feminist movement demanded such recognition, that 'by her life within the home, woman gives the State a support without which the common good cannot be achieved', and further provides that 'The State shall, therefore, endeavour to ensure that mothers shall not be obliged by economic necessity to engage in labour to the neglect of their duties in the home'. Article 41.3 contains a State pledge to 'guard with special care the institution of Marriage on which the Family is founded, and to protect it against attack'. Article 42 vests the right to educate children primarily in the parents, and Article 45, though it expressly states that the principles therein shall not be 'cognisable by any Court', declares a policy for the 'general guidance of the Oireachtas' that 'men and women equally have a right to an adequate means of livelihood'.

One might be forgiven for concluding from the above articles that women in Ireland enjoy an enviable position in comparison with their sisters in other jurisdictions which do not have written constitutions or which have written constitutions which do not enunciate women's rights in such terms. But constitutional articles are one thing; how they are interpreted and the extent to which they are availed of to vindicate rights are another. Until recently, the Irish constitutional courts[1] have rarely been invited to pronounce on these articles and, when invited, they have stopped short of interpreting them in a manner which might encourage women to undertake a programme of systematic challenge to sex discrimination. It is nevertheless true, as Gemma Hussey (currently Minister for Education) has said, that our constitutional courts have played a large part in the process of 'dragging Ireland kicking and screaming into the twentieth century'.[2]

In 1951 in In re Tilson Infants[3] the Supreme Court, reaffirming that the word 'parents' in Article 42 'naturally should include both the father and the mother',[4] interpreted Article 42 so as to end the common law rule of paternal supremacy and to replace it with joint parental authority in matters relating to the education of children. This case established the right of the mother to decide on how her children should be educated. In Murtagh Properties *v.* Cleary,[5] a case in which the barmen's union sought to prevent the employment of barwomen, the High Court held that the unnamed personal rights of the citizen under Article 40.3 of the constitution included the right of women to an adequate means of livelihood and that consequently 'a policy or general rule under which anyone seeks to prevent an employer from employing men or women on the ground of sex only is prohibited by the constitution'.[6] In McGee *v.* the Attorney-General[7] the Supreme Court, relying on Article 40.3 of the constitution, upheld a woman's right to the control of her own fertility, declaring that a denial of access to contraceptives was unconstitutional, and striking down Section 17 of the Criminal Law (Amendment) Act 1935, in so far as it made it a criminal offence for any person to sell, or import into Ireland for sale, any contraceptive. The right of access to information on contraception and fertility was vindicated in Irish Family Planning Association Ltd and Wilson *v.* Ryan[8] when a Censorship Board order prohibiting the sale and distribution of a booklet on contraception (sponsored by the association) as being indecent or obscene[9] was declared null and void, the order having been made in an unconstitutional manner.

The Juries Act 1927, to the extent that it provided that women were to be made exempt from jury service but entitled to serve on application, was held to be unconstitutional in De Búrca and Anderson *v.* the Attorney-General.[10] Until 1973 only three women had ever served on juries. Some discriminations against married women in the income tax code were removed as a result of the Supreme Court decision in Murphy *v.* the Attorney-General[11] that Sections 192-8 of the Income Tax Act 1967 were unconstitutional, in so far as they provided for the aggregation of the earned incomes of married couples with the result that penal rates of tax were levied on many married women. With the exception of the Tilson case, all of the above decisions were given in the last fifteen years.

It is doubtful whether many or any of the rights achieved by these cases would have been declared without resort to judicial proceedings. However, this is not to say that our constitutional courts have been in the vanguard of the struggle for equal rights. In some respects their decisions have inhibited the possibilities of exploiting constitutional articles to their full potential. In 1978, in Somjee *v.* the Minister for Justice and the Attorney-General,[12] a challenge to the constitutionality of the Irish Nationality and Citizenship Act 1956, which provides that an alien woman marrying an Irish man (other than a naturalised citizen) is automatically entitled at her option to Irish citizenship on marriage, whereas an alien man marrying an Irish woman is not, was unsuccessful. This discrimination was justified on the basis that 'the distinction is more properly regarded as confirming a form of privilege on female aliens rather than being invidiously discriminatory against male aliens'. Read another way, this means that Irish men marrying aliens are more privileged than Irish women so doing. The court found that the questioned sections of the Act do no more than provide a diversity of arrangements which is not prohibited by Article 40.1. An argument based on Article 9.1.2 of the constitution failed because the Act did not *exclude* male aliens from Irish nationality and citizenship by reason of their sex, though it was pointed out that the Minister for Justice in exercising his various discretions under the Act would not be acting in accordance with constitutional justice 'if he purported to refuse an application solely on the ground of the sex of the applicant'.

Apart from a refusal to outlaw what many could regard as a sex discrimination in the Somjee case, Irish judges, with perhaps three exceptions, have, despite several invitations, consistently refused to outlaw sex discrimination *per se* under Article 40.1. Instead, they have limited Article 40.1 to a mere 'acknowledgement of the human equality of all citizens',[14] a phrase which, although it does relate to the 'human attributes, or the ethnic, racial, social or religious background'[15] of citizens, and even their 'dignity as human beings',[16] does not include within those human attributes the gender of the citizen.

In all cases where women's rights have been upheld, the courts have done so, not by relying on Article 40.1 which might appear to be the most obvious article to rely on (particularly since it quite properly justifies reasonable discriminations), but by relying on other articles the scope of which, as judicially interpreted, does not allow for the development of an explicit constitutional doctrine prohibiting unreasonable sex discriminations. Thus in the Tilson case[17] the justification for vindicating a mother's right to educate her children was found in Article 42. In Murtagh Properties *v.* Cleary[18] a woman's right to an adequate means of livelihood and the unconstitutional invalidity of policies and rules preventing the employment of persons on the ground of sex alone was based on Article 40.3. The same Article 40.3 also provided the basis for the majority decision in McGee *v.* the Attorney-General[19] where the unnamed personal rights were held to include a right to marital privacy. In De Búrca and Anderson *v.* the Attorney-General[20] the majority of the Supreme Court, in holding that the conditional exclusion of women from the jury lists was unconstitutional, relied on Article 38.5. In Murphy *v.* the Attorney-General[21] the same court relied on Article 41.

In only three instances did individual judges rely on Article 40.1 to disapprove sex discriminations. Mr Justice Walsh in De Búrca and Anderson *v.* the Attorney-General[22] said that in his view 'it was not open to the State to discriminate in its enactments between persons who are subject to its laws solely on the grounds of the sex of those persons'. Mr Justice Keane in Somjee *v.* the Minister for Justice and the Attorney General[23] stated that the Minister for Justice in exercising a statutory discretion would not be acting in accordance with constitutional justice if he purported to refuse an application 'solely on the ground of the sex of the applicant', and Mr Justice Hamilton in the High Court decision in Murphy *v.* the Attorney-General[24] held that Section 192 of the Income Tax Act 1967 violated Article 40.1 because 'it discriminated invidiously against married couples and the husband in particular'.

None of these statements, however, form the main basis for the decisions in which they appear. Furthermore, even when conceding claims for various rights, the courts have frequently been at pains to limit the ambit of these rights. Thus, for example, Mr Justice Kenny in Murtagh Properties *v.* Cleary said that the guarantee in Article 40.1 had 'nothing to do with the trading activities of citizens or the conditions under which they are employed'.[25] Even when allowing that women had a right to an adequate means of livelihood, he was careful to limit that right by opining that differences in salary on the ground of sex would not be unconstitutional.[26] Thus the door was virtually closed on possibilities of achieving equal pay for equal work by constitutional action.

In McGee *v.* the Attorney-General,[27] the right of access to contraception, being based on a right to marital privacy, was thus limited to married persons and does not appear to be available as a constitutional right to single persons.[28] Furthermore, Mr Justice Griffin in the same case emphasised that his judgment was confined to 'contraceptives as such' and that 'it was not intended to apply to abortifacients, though called contraceptives'.[29] On this reading of that judgment, the right of access to contraceptives does not include the right to avail of the contraceptive of one's choice.

The failure by the courts to apply Article 40.1 or Article 40.3 to all unreasonable sex discriminations is a major disappointment. Together with the deterrent effect of enormously expensive legal costs and the strict requirements on *locus standi* for bringing proceedings alleging unconstitutionality,[30] it has meant that constitutional vindication of women's rights has been piecemeal and excessively dependent on the accidents of litigation.

While the constitutional courts have been prepared, when invited, to respond fairly positively in favour of women's rights, the same cannot be said of the Irish legislature where, ironically, there has been a sudden proliferation of women's rights statutes in the last fifteen years. These, however, were not passed because of some enlightened attitude towards the position of women in Irish society. Rather, most of them have been conceded in a reluctant manner as a response to various irresistible pressures. Three main factors have led to this sudden and welcome improvement in the law as it is applicable to women. The first was the re-emergence of a strong and articulate women's movement in the early 1970s, the second was Ireland's entry into the European Economic Community in January 1973, and the third the necessity of reacting to the judicial constitutional pronouncements already described.

The role of the women's movement in the achievement of better rights for women has not yet been adequately documented. It may, however, properly be said that, as a political force, it has mastered the art of political lobbying to the extent that its objectives are no longer dismissed or ignored by our predominantly male legislature. Particularly influential in the movement for law reform has been the Commission on the Status of Women, established by the government in March 1970 with the following terms of reference:

> To examine and report on the status of women in Irish society, to make recommendations on the steps necessary to ensure the participation of women on equal terms and conditions with men in the political, social, cultural and economic life of the country and to indicate the implications generally — including the estimated cost of such recommendations.

Membership of the commission was equally divided between women and men, and the appointees could by no means be labelled radical feminists. None the less, its first report in December 1972 contained no less than forty-nine detailed recommendations for improving women's rights in the areas of equal pay, employment generally, social welfare, marriage, taxation, juries, politics and public life, education and the home.[31] Two follow-up reports, in 1976 and 1978, by the Women's Representative Committee, established in 1974 by the then Minister for Labour, Michael O'Leary, monitored progress towards the implementation of the recommendations in the 1972 report and made suggestions for legislative and administrative reforms necessary for the improvement of women's rights.[32] The 1976 report detailed thirty-four recommendations and fifteen suggestions which had been implemented or partially implemented. By 1978 the committee was able to report that thirty-seven recommendations and fifteen suggestions had been implemented. There was still, however, a failure to improve women's rights in many areas, especially those relating to family planning, maternity leave, provision of creches, social welfare entitlements and taxation. In particular, it had been proved most difficult to change the laws where charges on the exchequer were involved. Since 1978, however, many of the outstanding reforms sought by the Commission for the Status of Women have been achieved.

There have been three main areas of legislative activity in the sphere of women's rights in the last decade. The first concerns the rights of women working outside the home. The Civil Service (Employment of Married Women) Act 1973 removed the ban on the recruitment or employment of married women in the civil service, local authorities and health boards. In 1974 the Anti-Discrimination (Pay) Act, which came into operation on 31 December 1975, established the right to equal pay for equal or like work and provided a system whereby this right may be attained and enforced. The Employment Equality Act 1977 is intended to ensure that a person's sex or marital status cannot be a determining factor with regard to access to vocational training, recruitment, work experience and promotional opportunities in employment. This Act also established the Employment Equality Agency, which is required to:

(a)   work towards the elimination of discrimination as between men and women in employment
(b)   promote equality of opportunity between men and women in relation to employment generally
(c)   keep under review both the Anti-Discrimination (Pay) Act 1974 and the Employment Equality Act 1977 and, whenever it thinks it necessary, to make proposals to the Minister for Labour for amending either or both of these Acts.[33]

The EEA has proved to be a most dynamic organisation, actively and genuinely committed to the promotion of equal rights for all.[34]

Protection of the rights of pregnant employees has also improved in recent years. The Unfair Dismissals Act 1977 accorded a limited amount of protection to pregnant workers against dismissal solely on the grounds of pregnancy or matters connected with it. The Employment Equality Act 1977 allowed employers to discriminate positively in favour of pregnant employees. But both fell short of granting a statutory right to pregnancy leave and job security for new mothers. This was provided by the long-awaited Maternity Protection for Employees Act 1981, which provides that female employees are entitled to maternity leave for a minimum period of fourteen weeks, to return to work after such leave, and to time off from work for ante-natal and post-natal care.

It would be a mistake to assume that all the above statutes originated solely from a desire to implement the recommendations of the

Commission on the Status of Women. In fact, their general motivation sprang from the necessity of implementing the EEC directives on equal pay[35] and on the equal treatment of men and women as regards access to employment, vocational training and promotion, and working conditions.[36]

The Finance Act 1980 secured a further improvement in the position of married women with their own incomes by providing, for the first time, that they could elect to be assessed and taxed in respect of their separate incomes and also by ensuring that, however married couples are taxed, they cannot become liable for more tax than two single people with the same combined incomes. This major reform was necessitated by the Supreme Court decision in Murphy *v.* the Attorney-General,[37] to the chagrin of the Minister for Finance.

The second major area of legislative reform was in respect of the rights of women in marriage. In 1970 the State recognised for the first time that it had a responsibility to provide support for deserted wives by enacting the Social Welfare Act, 1970, which established a scheme for deserted wives' allowances payable to deserted wives unable to obtain maintenance from their husbands.[38] The Social Welfare Act 1973 extended the scheme to make provision for the payment of a deserted wives' benefit payable under the same conditions as the allowance, except that there is no means test for the benefit which is financed out of insurance contributions.[39] A similar allowance became payable to the wives of prisoners under the Social Welfare (No. 2) Act 1974.[40] However, conditions regulating eligibility for these allowances are extremely strict, the sums payable are quite inadequate and the conditions of payment unnecessarily restrictive of the personal liberty of wives.

Some solution to the problem of separated wives and unsupported spouses and children was provided in The Family Law (Maintenance of Spouses and Children) Act 1976, under which a spouse who has failed to provide proper maintenance for his partner and/or children may be judicially compelled to do so. The enforcement machinery provided by this Act includes a right to attach the earnings of a maintenance debtor at source. The problem of errant husbands absconding to England, thereby evading their maintenance obligations, was partly solved by the Maintenance Orders Act 1974, which provides for a reciprocal enforcement of maintenance orders between Ireland and the United Kingdom. The Family Home Protection Act 1976 prohibits the legal owner of a family home (usually the husband) from selling it without the knowledge and consent of his spouse, though unfortunately it falls short of securing a joint legal right to ownership of the family home. The Family Law (Maintenance of Spouses and Children) Act 1976 *inter alia* empowers the court to make orders barring a spouse from the family home, thereby providing some relief to battered spouses. Further reforms in the law relating to family violence were implemented by the Violence and Matrimonial Procedures Act 1976 and the Family Law (Protection of Spouses and Children) Act 1981. The obnoxious court actions for criminal conversation, enticement and harbouring a spouse (actions based on the assumption that a wife was the property of her husband) were finally abolished by the Family Law Act 1981.

The credit for many of these reforms must be given to the various women's groups who campaigned for their implementation. Of these, particular credit must go to AIM, an organisation founded in 1972 with the specific objective of 'influencing the introduction of legislation to give Irish women and children an enforceable right in law to a proportion of the family income'. Two AIM reports on the need for family maintenance legislation (1972) and on legal separation (1976) considerably influenced much of the above legislation. The work of Women's Aid (an organisation for the support of battered wives and their children, now called Family Aid) alerted Irish society to the problems of family violence and was largely responsible for the legislative amelioration of the problems of battered wives.

The third area of legislative activity concerns what may be regarded as the rights of women generally including their rights *vis-à-vis* the State. Following the Supreme Court decision in De Búrca and Anderson *v.* the Attorney-General,[41] the Juries Act 1975 was passed so that all citizens, with a few special exceptions, are eligible for jury service irrespective of sex or property qualifications. The Health (Family Planning) Act 1979 finally grappled with the implications of the decision in McGee *v.* the Attorney-General[42] and required the Minister for Health to secure the organisation and provision of a comprehensive 'natural' family planning service, that is, a service concerned with family planning methods which do not involve the use of contraceptives. In contrast, health boards have a duty under the Health (Family Planning) Regulations 1980 to make available 'a family planning service' which phrase includes contraceptives. Although some of the provisions of this Act are farcical in the extreme,[43] it makes contraceptives (other than 'abortifacients') available to all women (married or unmarried), in theory at any rate.

Some reforms in the law and procedures relating to the rape of women (other than by their husbands) were introduced by the Criminal Law (Rape) Act 1981, though the Rape Crisis Centre, which campaigned most actively for law reform on rape, remains very dissatisfied with this Act.[44] Other notable reforms in the 1970s include improvements in the financial rights of unmarried mothers *vis-à-vis* the fathers of their children embodied in the Courts Act 1971[45] and the Family Law (Maintenance of Spouses and Children) Act 1976.[46] But these Acts provide support rights for illegitimate children only and not for their mothers who must rely on the Social Welfare Act 1973[47] which makes provision for the payment of a meagre allowance to unmarried mothers who can satisfy a means test.

While all the changes described above are welcome to a greater or lesser extent, many of them fall short of the full expectations and objectives of women who fought for or avail of them.[48] Space precludes an adequate discussion of their defects here. But defects there undoubtedly are — both in what they do and, perhaps more importantly, in what they fail to do. There still remains a large area of Irish law which must be reformed before it can truly be said that women's rights are properly protected.

Irish property law still ensures that married women are not given a fair opportunity for acquiring property and the psychological and economic independence this brings with it. True, a married woman is capable of owning and dealing with property in her own right[49] but she has no legal right to ownership of the family home or family property unless it is in her name or unless she contributed financially to its purchase.[50] Her contribution to the family by her work at home and the rearing of children does not entitle her to a share in her husband's wealth,[51] even when this is partly generated by State support like tax reliefs and house purchase grants which he obtains by virtue of his marriage to her. All her property rights (including those granted in the above-mentioned statutes) reflect her dependency: she has to go to her husband or the courts for support and shelter. Our law knows nothing of the system of community of property. It should be possible for the courts to develop this doctrine from the terms of the traditional marriage contract under which husbands 'endow' their wives with 'all they possess', from Article 41 of the constitution which expressly recognises the worth of the female and maternal role in the home, and from judicial pronouncements which appear to recognise that 'some preferential treatment of women citizens seems to be contemplated by the constitution'.[52] Disregard for the economic worth of women's work, and stereotyping of her socially perceived role, are further evidenced by the fact that a housewife suing for damages for personal injuries will not usually be compensated for loss of earning capacity because it is assumed she has none. The remarriage prospects of a widow claiming damages for the death of her husband are considered relevant when assessing the amount of damages awardable.

Despite repeated calls for reform, the domicile of the married Irish woman is determined by that of her husband whether she lives with him or not. One of the iniquitous effects of this rule is that under Irish law, Irish men may go abroad, acquire a foreign domicile, and divorce their wives, but Irish women may not. Divorce is still constitutionally prohibited in Ireland.[53] Women are deprived of entitlement to many social welfare allowances and benefits either because they have not been allowed to, or have not been in a position to, pay social welfare contributions, or because it is assumed that they are (or should be) dependent on men. Thus, for example, unemployment benefits/assistance are paid to the husband whether he be a drunkard or a tyrant. Even where wives have paid contributions in their own right, unemployment benefits or allowances to which they are entitled are less extensive and granted on different (and more stringent) terms than those available to men. The social welfare system is founded on the philosophy that women are dependent on men and that society must only support them when this dependence (for one reason or another) ceases.

But of course law reform is not the only important aspect of the problem of sex discrimination. If the law is to play an effective part it must be associated with changes in social attitudes. There is some evidence that the climate of opinion concerning the status and relations of the sexes has undergone a favourable change in the last fifteen years. Faced with women competing for jobs and promotion, men have suddenly come to understand the housewife's true value. It is no longer politically acceptable to speak of the 'non-working' wife: she has become 'the woman who works in the home'. Farms have become 'family farms'. Election programmes persuading woman to elect men to the Oireachtas have their chapters on the position of women. Securing a more widespread and fundamental change in social attitudes to the position of women in Irish society is the task, and the challenge, of the eighties.

Postscript

Since this article was written there have been a number of developments which continue to reflect changing attitudes in Irish society towards women's rights. These include the appointment of a Minister for Women's Affairs and the setting up of Joint Oireachtas Sub-Committees on Marriage Breakdown and Women's Rights. The Minister for Education, Gemma Hussey, has initiated a programme for the abolition of sexism in education. EEC Directive 79/7/EEC on equal treatment for men and women in matters of social security[54] is to be implemented in 1985. Perhaps the most dramatic development of all in the long term has been the declaration in O'G *v.* the Attorney-General[55] that sex discrimination may be unconstitutional under Article 40.1 of the constitution. This long-awaited declaration (ironically obtained by a man) may well be the foundation for many future challenges to sex discriminations.

Notes

1 There are no separate constitutional courts in Ireland. The expression here used refers to the High and Supreme Courts where the constitutional rights discussed in this chapter were asserted.
2 *The Irish Times*, 26 January 1980.
3 In re Tilson Infants (1951) I.R. 1. The joint rights of parents to the custody of their children were not enshrined in legislation until the Guardianship of Infants Act 1964.
4 *Ibid.*, 32.
5 Murtagh Properties *v.* Cleary (1972) I.R. 330.
6 *Ibid.*, 336.
7 McGee *v.* the Attorney-General (1974) I.R. 284.
8 Irish Family Planning Association *v.* Ryan (1979) I.R. 295.

9 The court expressed grave doubts about whether the booklet could properly be described as being 'indecent or obscene'. O'Higgins, C.J., in his judgment (p. 315) said that 'Far from being pornographic or lewdly commercial or pandering to prurient curiosity, it simply aimed at giving basic factual information on a delicate topic as to which there is genuine concern.'

10 De Búrca and Anderson *v.* the Attorney-General (1976) I.R. 38. The plaintiffs in this case are two leading feminists.

11 Murphy *v.* the Attorney-General, S.C. 25 January 1980. The writer modestly claims some of the credit for organising the challenge to the constitutionality of the Income Tax Act 1967.

12 Somjee *v.* the Minister for Justice and the Attorney-General, H.C. 20 December 1979.

13 Walsh, J., in De Búrca and Anderson *v.* the Attorney-General (1976) I.R. 38, p. 71; Keane, J., in Somjee *v.* the Minister for Justice and the Attorney-General, H.C. 20 December 1979; Hamilton, J., in Murphy *v.* the Attorney-General, H.C. 12 October 1979.

14 See e.g. Murtagh Properties *v.* Cleary (1972) I.R. 330; De Búrca and Anderson *v.* the Attorney-General (1976) I.R. 38.

15 The State (Nicholaou *v.* An Bord Uchtála (1966) I.R. 565, p. 639. Quinn's Supermarket *v.* the Attorney-General (1972) I.R., 1, pp 13, 14.

16 De Búrca and Anderson *v.* the Attorney-General (1976) I.R. 38.

17 In re Tilson Infants (1951) I.R. 1.

18 Murtagh Properties *v.* Cleary (1972) I.R. 330.

19 McGee *v.* the Attorney-General (1974) I.R. 284.

20 De Búrca and Anderson *v.* the Attorney-General (1976) I.R. 38.

21 Murphy *v.* the Attorney-General, S.C. 25 January 1980.

22 De Búrca and Anderson *v.* the Attorney-General (1976) I.R. 38 at 71.

23 Somjee *v.* Minister for Justice and the Attorney-General, H.C. 20 December 1979.

24 Murphy *v.* the Attorney-General, H.C. 12 October 1979.

25 Murtagh Properties *v.* Cleary (1972) I.R. 330, p. 337.

26 *Ibid.*, 336.

27 McGee *v.* the Attorney-General (1974) I.R. 284.

28 *Ibid.*, 314, 315, 325, 326, 333, 336. See G. Whyte, Haughey's Family Planning Act, 'Waiting to be Challenged', *Case*, Feb/April 1980.

29 McGee *v.* the Attorney-General (1974) I.R. 284, p. 335.

30 See e.g. Norris *v.* the Attorney-General, H.C. 10 October 1980; Cahill *v.* Sutton, S.C. 9 July 1980.

31 Report of the Commission on the Status of Women (1972) (Prl. 2760).

32 Progress Report on the implementation of the Recommendations in the Report of the Commission on the Status of Women (1976); Second Progress Report on the implementation of the Recommendations in the Report of the Commission on the Status of Women (1978).

33 Employment (Equality) Act 1977, Section 35.

34 See Annual Reports of the Employment Equality Agency 1978-80.

35 EEC Directive 75/117/EEC. OJ No L45, 19 February 1975.

36 EEC Directive 76/207/EEC. OJ No L39, 14 January 1976.

37 Murphy *v.* the Attorney General S.C. 25 January 1980.

38 See now Social Welfare (Consolidation) Act.1981.

39 *Ibid.*

40 *Ibid.*

41 De Búrca and Anderson *v.* the Attorney-General (1976) I.R. 38.

42 McGee *v.* the Attorney-General (1974)'I.R. 284.

43 See A. Shatter, *Family Planning Irish Style* (1978) which gives a humorous account of the potential effects of the Health (Family Planning) Bill 1978.

44 See Second Report of Rape Crisis Centre (1981).

45 Courts Act 1971, Section 19.

46 Family Law (Maintenance of Spouses and Children) Act 1976, Part IV.
47 See now Social Welfare (Consolidation) Act 1981.
48 See e.g. Annual Reports of the Employment Equality Agency, 1978-80; EEC Commission Report on the situation at 12 August 1980 with regard to the implementation of the directive on equal treatment for men and women; suggestions for reform in Shatter (1981); Second Report of the Rape Crisis Centre (1981); Commission on the Status of Women, *Irish Women Speak Out* (1981).
49 Married Women's (Status) Act 1957.
50 Conway *v.* Conway (1976) I.R. 254.
51 R.K. *v.* M.K., H.C. 10 October 1978, in which Finlay, P., stated: 'The extent of her [the wife's] work in the household and in the care of children was very considerable but our law does not recognise so far at least a right arising from that type of work to a part ownership of any family or marriage property.'
52 See e.g. O'Higgins, C.J., in De Búrca and Anderson *v.* the Attorney-General (1976) I.R. 38, p. 61.
53 *Constitution of Ireland*, Article 41.3.2. See J. Kelly *The Irish Constitution*, (1980), pp 487-92.
54 EEC Directive 79/7/EEC 05 NOL/64, 19 December 1978.
55 High Court, 1 March 1984.

Further reading

Arnold & Kirkby (eds), *The Abortion Referendum — The case against*, Dublin 1982.
Duncan, 'Supporting the Institution of Marriage in the Republic of Ireland', in Eehelaar & Katz *Marriage and Cohabitation in Contemporary Societies* 1980, Ch. 9.
Duncan, *The Case for Divorce in the Republic of Ireland*, Irish Council for Civil Liberties, Dublin 1982.
Commission on the Status of Women: *Irish Women Speak Out* Dublin 1981.
Report of the Commission on the Status of Women (1972) Prl. 2760.
Kelly, *The Irish Constitution* 2nd ed Dublin. 1984.
Margaret MacCurtain & Donncha Ó Corráin (eds). *Women in Irish Society* Dublin 1979.
Alan Shatter, *Family Law in the Republic of Ireland*, Dublin 1981.

The Female Song in the Irish Tradition

Nóirín Ní Riain

It is necessary in discussing feminine creativity in song to confine observations to the subjective feminine song — the song composed *by* the
woman rather than one composed *about* her. This female song-type has
far fewer survivals than the male-composed song. Two distinct sources
united in the compilation of the repertoire of feminine songs to be drawn
upon here: firstly, research I recently carried out on religious song, and
secondly, personal interpretation as I have experienced it within this
repertoire. These two sources overlapped when the academic research reinforced intuitive ideas arising from interpretation.

The Feminine Repertoire

I have confined the material used here to the Irish language and,
although it would be naive to claim that my repertoire of female songs in
this language is exhaustive, I have drawn from all sources of traditional
Irish folk music and have selected a representative collection of songs
from each.[1]

The use of the terms 'masculine' and 'feminine' in this tradition is
essentially different from that used in the tradition of European Art
music, where they are conventional terms concerning cadential endings
and technical theme labelling. Here we are concerned with actual sexual
difference.

I believe that fundamental features of the woman's song, particularly
in the Irish language, display in the musical structure a certain distinctive-
ness from the male song. These musical values of feminity, however, are
in no way confined to the female song. If this were so, then the entire
corpus of woman's song would have been categorised and neatly shelved
away long before now. Textual distinctions speak clearly for themselves
and any distinction between the poetry of the two sexes, as it is isolated
from the music, must remain for discussion by the linguist. For the
musicologist, words serve as signposts to the feminine musical imagination by enunciating the peculiarly female composition.

The living song depends upon a performance and upon the interpretation of the singer. The musical nuances assume various guises with each

singer and, whereas in almost all cases the words remain intact from singer to singer, musical expression varies according to the singer. This discussion incorporates concepts not only of feminine creativity within the songs but also within the singer, the two being linked inseparably in any folk tradition.

Two factors determine this musical experience of the singer. By far the more mundane factor is the singer's dexterity and her technical ability to use her voice in any song, regardless of the identification which she may feel with it. Technical competence can easily be acquired, but this is not enough for the traditional singer's performance of living song: each performance must be unique and each performance must be vital. And this is where the second factor comes in: in order to achieve this the singer must have a depth of understanding of both the sentiments expressed in the text of the song and of the wedding of the music and text. The tunes to which these texts are wedded were composed very much in the mood of the poem in question. Since this is so, the female song repertory must be studied in three aspects: the text, the music and their interaction.

Songs of Work

The work songs are easily described in two broad categories. The first are those songs composed by the woman within the home which are nearly always related to her role as mother and child-rearer. Two maternal song-types emerge. The first tends to be soothing, hypnotic and tranquillising and is used as a lullaby. A typical example would be the song 'Seoithín Seó'.[2] The second maternal song-type is metrical, vigorous and vivacious and is used as a dandling song. The function of both these types largely dictates their structure and movement: in the first case the infant is lulled to sleep in the cradle; in the second the child is awake and demanding affection through physical contact.

The second category of work songs are those composed and performed during such activities as spinning, weaving or herding. Spinning and weaving were social functions, and so the construction of these songs caters for group participation. This is illustrated by such songs as 'Im Bim Baboro', 'S'ambo éara' and 'Ailiú Éanaí[3] where the first and last phrases of the three-phase construction are sung by everyone while the middle phrase is sung by one person.

With the exception of one herding song, all occupational songs echo the rhythm of the work in hand. Herding is not a particularly social activity and therefore does not require such rhythmic synchronisation. It does produce the same three-phrase structure but in a song that is rhythmically freer and very much more ornamented. Keeping the cattle in the pasture and away from corn, in what was for the majority of families a very tiny patch of land, seems to have been an almost exclusively feminine task.[4]

Cáit Ní Ghallchóir, traditional singer (Photograph, 'Irish Press')

Female work songs, whether maternal, social or solitary, are striking for the onomatopaeic quality of even the nonsense syllables, which mostly adorn the first and third lines. Just as the music seems to be tailor-made for the activity in hand, so the phrases such as 'cucanandy' or 'digeas o deamhas' complement the music of the dandling song, and 's'ambo éara bhuilibo éara' recreates the sound of the spinning wheel.

Songs of Desire

Of the three categories described here, the largest body is that described as 'songs of desire', particularly those which relate stories of the woman, sometimes unrequited in love and sometimes the distraught victim of the match-maker. It is significant that in the case of the latter, where the young woman describes her withered impotent spouse and longs for her young virile lover, the song is metrical and very often has a chorus.[5] These songs are therefore essentially social and were intended to be heard and reacted to as well as expressing a deep personal frustration.

An example of the genre is 'Fuigfidh mise an baile seo' (I quote the second and fourth stanzas):

'Mhuire, nach mé'n trua 's mé pósta ar a' sclábhaí,
Nach ligeann amach chun Aifrinn mé lá saoire ná Dé Domhnaigh,
Nach dtéann go tigh a' leanna lion 's nach n-ólfadh gine óir liom,
'S nach dteannfadh lena chroí mé mar 'dhéanfadh an buachaill óg
liom!

. . .

Pósadh go hóg mé mar gheall ar na puntaí,
Lán mo dhá láimh is níor shásaigh sé riamh m' intinn;
Nach trua nach dtig an reacht 'mach mar tá ar bha 's ar chaoirigh,
An té nach dtaitneodh 'mhargadh leis a sheoladh ar ais 'un aonaigh!

(Am I not a pity now, married to a wretch
That won't let me out to Mass on a holy day or Sunday,
That won't come to the alehouse and drink a golden guinea
Or press me to his heart as a young fellow would do!

. . .

They married me young for the sake of the money
I had my fill of it and I was never happy;
A pity we can't choose as we can with sheep or cattle:
If you don't like your bargain you can go back to the market!)

Female love songs describing the beloved objectively or expressing fulfillment in love are extremely rare. Tensions, conflicts of desire and unrealised relationships, because of either parental interference or unacknowledged love due to absence or death, were the essential inspiration for female creativity. An excessive obsession with oneself as opposed to the beloved is very evident, although this would appear to be the typically western response of the love-stricken woman.[6] This narcissism excludes any adequate account of the loved one. However, two aspects of the physique are frequently mentioned — the hair and the eyes.

The intense passionate bitter outcry of frustrated desire is not only expressed through the texts. The music to which these words are wedded mirrors the sentiments in a very subtle manner. It is relatively easy to detect and define the technique of 'word painting' in European Art music. Yet a perception of interaction between sentiments or emotions and music is very much more dependent on both the individual who performs it and the person who listens to it being performed. Two songs of desire best represent this interaction.

'Dónal Og'[7] — a song of love unrequited which was common to many areas of Ireland and Scotland — has been loudly proclaimed as one of the finest Irish folk texts:

(Dónal Og, if you cross the water,
Take me with you and don't forget,
And you'll get a present each fair and market day
And the King of Greece's daughter to share your bed.)

The tune appears to be a simple four-phrase melody. Although each is different, the phrases grow out of one another, extending the musical idiom and range. The first two phrases are heralding the climax which centres around the high note, D, in phrases three and four. Then the climax subsides to mirror the quiet despair of the text. The musical form

— A B C D (four different phrases) — is not as inevitable as the regular binary and ternary forms for the learner. These regular forms are based upon phrase repetition and are more easily assimilated both by the listener and the singer.

The second striking song of desire, although expressing a very different emotional feeling and setting, uses its musical idiom to heighten the intensity in a similar way. The Donegal song, 'Fill, fill, a rún ó'[9] encapsulates the frantic, irrational thoughts of the eighteenth-century mother shattered by her son's leaving the Catholic priesthood to become a Protestant minister, and her uncontrolled feelings are crystallised not only by the spontaneous words but also by an appropriate musical blend.

Dhiúltaigh tú Peadar is Pól
Mar gheall ar an óir is an airgid
Dhiúltaigh tú Bainríon na Glóire
Agus d'iompaigh tú 'gcóta an mhinistéir.

(Return, return my dear
Return my dear and do not depart,
Return to me, pulse of my heart,
The Queen of Glory awaits you

You renounced Peter and Paul
For the sake of gold and silver,
You renounced the Queen of Glory
And donned the traitorous coat of a minister.)

In this Donegal song, a verse is wedded to three phrases, which in itself seems to be a particularly feminine construction since, as already pointed out, many female work songs consist of three phrases. However, each phrase, as in 'Dónal Óg', is unique and only related to the others in so far as it represents a logical growth and entity. Although the number of phrases in the two songs varies, the form of these phrases is similar — A B C D and A B C. Both songs are in hexatonic, Ionian mode with the fourth note of the scale consistently omitted. Both songs have a precisely similar range of a ninth. It is rare in Irish folk music for two songs which are definitely not variants of one another to have so many features in common.

The overall power and structure of these two songs of desire when compared with other female songs, such as songs of work or indeed even the songs composed by the match-maker's victim, are introverted and personal. It is not fanciful to say that these two songs were essentially solo conceptions: it would appear that just one person composed the song — in many of the cumulative work songs, collective improvisation apparently took place and the social setting was very important. The social performance for the song-type of 'Dónal Óg' and 'Fill, fill a rún ó' was irrelevant. In the broadest sense, this song-type is exclusive of others — there is no chorus and there is no musical repetition. The complexity of feelings in both the texts and the music is narcissistic and non-altruistic.

There is an overlap in female creativity between the social and non-social song. The maternal song — 'Fill, fill a rún ó' — provides the link between the social and non-social functions of songs of desire, songs of work and songs of prayer. The opening phrase dramatically forces itself upon the listener like a loud hysterical shriek. Beginning on the high note, F, which only figures in the first two phrases, and sung to the shrill reiterated 'fill' in the first and last verses, can have a strong hypnotic effect on the listener. One wonders how strongly this mother was influenced by the musical technique of the keen — a practice which she no doubt would have carried out many times. The sparse, musical remnants of the keening woman consistently emphasise the importance of this powerful high note, eliciting a compulsive, irresistible concentration not only from the audience but also from the singer.

An Caoineadh

Cað a _____ dhéan-faiðh mé _____

Tá tú   ar   shiúl _____ uaim

A - gus   air   -   iú _____

A -gus an-uir ~   -   -   iðh

níl duin' ar bith _____ a~ gam

'Sair~   -   -   -   iú

A - gus   mé _____ liomféin

Dá mbei-theá go moch _____ a ~ gam

A-gus och! och! och- ón air ~ iú gan   thú

Songs of Prayer

Religious song in Irish comprises three strands: eighteenth-century religious poetry by known poets which was sung to popular airs of the time; poetry which was artificially wedded to unrelated folk tunes; and finally, authentic folk songs where the text and tune were collected simultaneously. It is the traditional religious folk song which is relevant here.

Within this small body of traditional song, there are songs created to be sung with others and songs created as a personal expression of faith. But even within the personal songs, the texts are not subjective and introverted in the same way as in the songs of desire. Here the musical interaction is integral in conveying the intense feelings reminiscent of both the songs of desire and the keen.

Categorically pronouncing upon a folk tradition is always dangerous. While recognising this danger it is possible, with a little imagination, to interpret the songs in the following way. The texts are centred on Mary, which does not in itself necessarily imply a feminine composer. However, two aspects of this emphasis on Mary are significantly feminine: the understanding of and identification with Mary in her role as mother — she is sometimes addressing her infant who is now a man being crucified, and she is sometimes sharing his life with him — and the keening element: many of these songs vividly relate the death of Christ, thus providing in the eyes of the Irish woman a keening situation. The ritual of the pagan keen is now re-enacted musically, motivated by Christian religious fervour.

The social and non-social songs mingle very naturally. In England, the numerical carol-type 'The Seven Joys of Mary' and 'The Seven Sorrows of Mary' were supposedly composed by the Franciscans as a method of popular instruction in the thirteenth century.[11] Repeated texts and chorus figure prominently in those songs for this purpose. The three intact versions of this carol found in Ireland are constructed upon this form and although the tunes in themselves are very distinctive, they cannot be said to heighten or add to the textual sentiments.

One Connemara version of 'Seacht nDólás na Maighdine Muire'[12] defies this theory':

> *An chéad dólás do bhí ar an Maighdéan nuair a tóiríodh a leanbh,*
> *Caipíní dubha air 's na Giúdaigh á ghreadadh.*
> *Ailliliú ó 'Iosa, ailliliú is tú mo leanbh,*
> *Ailliliú ó 'Iosa, is tú Rí geal na bhFlaitheas.*
> (Mary's first sorrow when they persecuted her child
> Black caps upon him and the Jews striking him.
> *Ailliliú* O Jesus, *ailliliú* my child,
> *Ailliliú* O Jesus, you are heaven's king.)

Textually, the three-line verse form is A B C (chorus). A and C remain static throughout the subsequent verses. When wedded to the music, this text assumes an intense emotional, keen-like quality which places it in the realm of the keen and the non-social song of desire. This is perhaps the prime example of the power of the music upon the text.

A close variant of this same tune is sung to the text of 'Caoine na dTrí Muire'[13] by the same singer. Sorcha Ní Ghuairim, the singer, calls it 'Caoine Mhuire' and although many religious songs bear the title 'Caoine', none resembles the keen musically as closely as 'Caoine Mhuire'.

Caoine Mhuire — as sung by Sorcha Ní Ghuairim

A Pheadair !as-pail 'A bhfaca tú mo ghrá geal?

Och - ón Agus och - ón ó!

A Pheadair 'aspail, an bhfaca tú mo ghrá geal?
M'ochón agus m'ochón ó!
Chonaic me ar ball é i lár a námhad.
M'ochón agus m'ochón ó!

Cé hé an fear breá sin ar chrann na Páise?
M'ochón agus m'ochón ó!
An é nach n-aithníonn tú do mhac, a mháthair?
M'ochón agus m'ochón ó!

An é sin an maicín d'iompair mé trí ráithe?
M'ochón agus m'ochón ó!
Nó an é sin an maicín a rugadh sa stábla?
M'ochón agus m'ochón ó!

(Peter, apostle, have you seen my darling?
M'ochón agus m'ochón ó!
I saw him just now and his enemies around him
M'ochón agus m'ochón ó!

Who is that fine man on the Tree of Passion?
M'ochón agus m'ochón ó!
Do you not recognise your son, dear mother?
M'othón agus m'ochón ó!

Is that the little son I carried three seasons?
M'ochón agus m'ochón ó!
Is that the little son that I bore in the stable?
M'ochón agus m'ochón ó!)

The tune has two distinct phrases, the first beginning on the highest
note of the song, which is in hexatonic, Ionian mode with the fourth
degree missing. These musical features are similar to the two songs of
desire discussed. Although the *ochón agus ochón ó* acts as a refrain textually, the complexity of the fragment to which it is sung dictates a solo
rather than a group performance.

The whole question of performance comes up when discussing religious songs. Were they associated with any church ceremony or ritual? There is no evidence to suggest that any of these folk songs were sung as part of church worship. Diarmuid Ó Laoghaire recalls hearing 'Seacht nDólás na Maighdine Muire' being recited after the rosary each evening in the 1940s. Certainly, the social religious song interferes little with the performer or listener and, like the rosary, is binding and mechanical and bears repetition. 'Dónal Óg', 'Fill, fill a rún ó' and 'Caoine Mhuire', on the other hand, would hardly have been sung repeatedly by the woman after her first passionate outcry when creating the song and giving everything to its impulse — an obsession with love, possessiveness or piety.

Since it is likely that religious songs are the oldest folk songs to have survived, they also reveal the oldest examples of feminine musical creativity.

Conclusion

Female expression in Irish traditional song can be divided into two musical streams: a song-type which exhibits a social element in the broadest sense, and a song-type which is essentially a solitary, sometimes narcissistic exercise. The textual categories of female song discussed above merge within these two streams, each category exposing social and non-social examples.

Basically, the social song, whether it be work song, love song or religious song of praise, has certain strong musical features. The presence of musical and textual repetition in these songs indicates group participation. This repetition is incorporated, sometimes in the form of a chorus, sometimes in the form of a reiterated phrase. A metrical tempo facilitates the transmission of song to others and this tempo is consistent in all the social songs discussed. A textual chorus does not necessarily define a social song. However, a definable tempo, regardless of its accompanying text, seems to indicate a less personal mode of expression.

The solitary song, on the other hand, excludes ensemble performance through the intricacy of the music. Textual repetition appears frequently but it is within the music, and indeed its performance, that this non-social song stands apart. The free tempo, a regular feature in these songs, makes ensemble singing practically impossible and the phrase construction, where repetition is rare, indicates a mildly misanthropic expression.

The corpus of female traditional songs is unmistakably smaller than its male counterpart. Two factors contribute to this paucity of feminine repertoire. Firstly, the female song is idiosyncratic; each expression is musically unique, never presenting a reproduction. Because of the intensity and exigence which is integral, the female song is less frequently created. Secondly, since many of the songs are essentially an introverted creativity, the social performance situation is less important. Women primarily used song as a medium for release of deeply personal tensions and frustrations, thus fewer female songs were heard, transmitted or preserved.

Music transcribed by Nóirín Ní Riain. Music copyist: Dom Kevin Healy, OSB.

Notes

1 Nóirín Ní Riain 'The Music of Traditional Religious Songs in Irish', MA thesis UCC, 1980, Preface, i-iii.
2 *Óró Damhnaigh*, LP recording, Gael Linn, 1977, Side 2, Band 4.
3 *Ibid*. Side 1, Band 3: *Deora Aille*, LP recording, Claddagh, CC6, Side 2, Band 4,: *Óró Damhnaigh*, Side 1, Band 3.
4 *World Library of Folk and Primitive Music: Ireland*. Folkways, SL-204, LP recording notes to Band 12, Side 1.
5 Three examples of this song-type are: 'Fuigfidh mise an baile seo', 'An seanduine', 'An seanduine cam'.
6 Evelyne Sullerot, *Women On Love*, The Chaucer Press, Suffolk, 1979.
7 *Deora Aille*, Side 2, Band 1.
8 The music transcriptions throughout this article represent my own interpretation of the songs and are not accurate transcriptions from the recordings chosen.
9 *Deora Aille*, Side 1, Band 2.
10 'The Music of Traditional Religious Song in Irish'; see note 4 above.
11 *The Folk Carol of England*, Douglas Brice, London, 1967, p. 78.
12 Tape Archive, Department of Irish Folklore, UCD, Sorcha Ní Ghuairim, 1940.
13 Tape Archive, English Institute of Recorded Sound, London, Sorcha Ní Ghuairim, 1956.
14 An tAthair Diarmuid O'Laoghaire, S.J., *Muire Mór*, Dublin, 1959, p. 78.

Irish Lace and Irish Crochet

Mary Coleman

George Pellew, an American visitor to Ireland in 1887, noted that in one of the 'Big Houses' where he stayed his 'hostess drew herself the most delicate designs for the lacework of the tenants' daughters'.[1] Thus he draws attention to an important aspect of the history of Irish lace — the patronage of the ascendancy in the eighteenth and nineteenth centuries.

Louisa Meredith draws attention to another important aspect — Irish poverty made Irish lace. She observes:

> To know the Irish poor is to know Ireland. Poverty is the national characteristic. It is the poor that constitute the distinguishing element of the country; their spirit rules in its agitations, and dictates all its claims. They are the seething mass in its economy; they work, and they achieve too, not fortune but fame.[2]

Mrs Meredith has in mind the enormous popularity Irish lace had achieved by the end of the nineteenth century. For the thousands of women workers 'at the sewing' by candlelight in their mud cabins or out of doors in soft weather the fame was an anonymous one: few names of individual lacemakers survive. We know that they were many (Ben Lindsey names twenty-seven lace centres in 1886), and we know something of their sufferings and the diseases to which they fell victim. But their history is not exclusively a gloomy one. A present-day lacemaker, Mrs Eithne D'Arcy of Roslea in County Fermanagh, remembers her grandmother's accounts of the social aspect of lacemaking, the gaiety of summer meetings and winter nights when friends met to chat, exchange news and 'be at the sewing' and how 'the workers each would come round and they would go to Mrs So and So one night and would all congregate and they would have a good old chatter. It was great social life.' Mrs Meredith later in her book reminds us of the great development of lacemaking which followed in answer to the privations of the Famine of 1847:

> A perfect clamour for employment arose. To satisfy this, a most remarkable movement took place. Women of the upper ranks developed an extraordinary skill in needlework and also a great

commercial aptitude to turn it to a profitable account. The repose of aristocratic society and the leisure of the cloister were disturbed. Ladies burst the bonds of conventionalisms, and went regularly into business to procure remunerative occupation for the destitute of their own sex. The female children of the poor all over the land became the subjects of instruction in the making up of various sorts of articles for sale.[4]

By 1853 schools had been established throughout the country and forty-six of them exhibited their work in Dublin in that year. Two kinds of goods were on show: the well-established 'sewed muslin' and crochet lace. Crochet lace marked a new departure, and for its distinction of execution it was to receive the name *Point d'Irlande* later in the century. I will return to consideration of the technique of Irish laces later. For the present, I propose to examine the story of lace before the Famine; it is a story that begins in the eighteenth century, and it is closely linked with the history of the Dublin Society founded in 1731 for the encouragement of crafts and the advancement of knowledge.[5]

The Dublin Society awarded many prizes for skill in lacemaking and was active in its promotion. Both needle point (chiefly imitation of foreign models) and 'bone lace' (as bobbin lace was then described) were produced. Two enlightened patrons, Dr Madden in the early decades of the century and Lady Arbella Denny in the later, are remembered for their philanthropic contributions. Dr Madden established premiums for teaching lacemaking and records survive of these for the period 1743—56. The Dublin Society then supplemented the Madden premiums and gave the administration of the awards to Lady Arbella Denny who was especially involved with the lacemaking activity of the Foundling Hospital in Dublin. It is not possible to assess the quality of this lace as no certain examples have survived.

This record of collaboration between 'Big House' and mud cabin provides a grace note in the general climate of oppression which marked eighteenth-century Ireland when the barriers of class and religion established two communities, one colonial and Protestant placed in privilege and power, the other native and Catholic placed in subjection and poverty. With the Act of Union of 1801 which abolished the Irish Parliament, large numbers of the ascendancy left for London. The splendour of vice-regal occasions was diminished and the call for lace to adorn dress and uniform was less urgent. It was not until the second decade of the new century that lacemaking received a new impetus, and it received it first in the north where of four chief centres (Ardee, Carrickmacross, Clones and Inishmacsaint) it was Carrickmacross which was to emerge as one of the four leading 'schools' of Irish lace. The remaining three are Limerick, Youghal and Irish Crochet.

Carrickmacross (not technically a lace but appliqué on net) was introduced here by Mrs Grey Porter, wife of the Rector of Donaghmoyne, and her maid Anne Steadman, who are reported to have been fascinated by Italian specimens of appliqué and who set out to copy them. The increased availability of machine net which was cheap and of breadths suitable for veils and shawls was a special boost to their efforts. Mrs Porter can claim the honour of innovating, of adapting an ancient art in response to new material. It was, however, her neighbour, Miss Reid of Rahans who established Carrickmacross on a commercial basis. Miss Reid and her sister Dora built a schoolhouse on their property for the teaching of lace which was officially confined to their tenants but in which, no doubt, others took part.

Their commissions came from private sources and it appears that as these declined the Reid enterprise suffered a quiet extinction. But the making of Carrickmacross lace continued as a 'cottage industry' and in 1846 a Mr Tristran Kennedy, estate manager to the Bath and Shirley properties on which the town stands, built seven schools with one central school which later supplied teachers and designers to the others, and

Youghal handkerchief, National Museum of Ireland

developed orders.

Kennedy was successful in obtaining a grant of £100 in 1850 from the Privy Council of Trade to open a training class for young girls in drawing and designing for 'the Lace Manufacture in certain Industrial Schools in that district', and he was commended by Lord Clarendon, the Lord Lieutenant, in 1852 for his success in associating industrial and literacy training in his model schools. On Kennedy's election to Parliament in 1852, he continued his patronage of Carrickmacross by acting, in effect, as PRO in London. His success can be measured by his obtaining an order from Queen Victoria — the lace was described as 'beau travail' at the Paris Exhibition of 1855, and it was not till 1872 that it was known officially as 'Carrickmacross'.

The years between had been years of steady progress. The Bath and Shirley School was fortunate in its succession of good teachers, and they were aware of the need for good designs, and on occasion obtained them from students of the Dublin School of Art. Kennedy had also introduced Brussels lace. There was, it is true, some decline in the fineness of workmanship and the availability of cheap machine-made lace presented a strong challenge. This led to some decline in the Bath and Shirley enterprise as the century came to a close, but Carrickmacross found a powerful new impetus through the founding there of St Louis Convent in 1860, which remains to this day the focus of the tradition.

The founding of St Louis Convent highlights a development which had earlier marked a new stage in the history of Irish laces. This development was the gradual transfer of patronage from private and ascendancy hands to religious and commercial enterprise. It was in Limerick, one of the great 'schools' of Irish lace, that the commercial development began. In 1829 Charles Walker (whose wife owned a lace firm) established a centre with twenty-four workers from Nottingham. Nottingham was already well-known as a lace centre (drawing its artistic inspiration from Lille) and as manufacturer of machine-made lace, and both were to determine the style of Limerick lace. It is, like Carrickmacross, essentially 'enrichment' of an existing material. Walker, we are informed, was 'evidently a kind and popular employer, and he and his teachers found such apt and clever pupils in the Limerick of that day that the industry soon took firm root'.[6]

Those 'apt and clever pupils' had then small choice of alternative employment and while Walker's company provided a source of welcome finance there can be no doubt that commercial exploitation was present too. Irish labour was cheap labour. Workers were paid from three to seven shillings weekly and their work fetched from eight shillings to over a pound a piece. The historian Elizabeth Boyle remarks: 'The prices were low, but not ruinously low.'[7] Certainly, Walker was not operating at a loss.

Other entrepeneurs moved into Limerick. A Mr Greaves, for example, founded a factory in 1836 which employed over two hundred workers. Limerick town itself with its ancient castle, cathedral, Georgian houses, and spacious mall, provided an agreeable ambiance for this luxury item. But with the death of Walker in 1842 a decline in the industry began. The decline was partly due to the inferior designs in use, which deteriorated through excessive repetition. And the decline must be measured in artistic rather than commercial terms. Limerick lace, though not of the first quality, still found buyers. However, a contributor to *The Irish Homestead* in 1897 suggested reasons for the decline of the demand in commercial terms also: 'the Court mourning caused by the death of the Prince Consort . . . and the introduction of beautiful and inexpensive machine-made lace at Nottingham'.[8] If this is to be accepted it is a superb instance of the daughter destroyed by the mother.

Such destruction, happily, was not total. The revival of Limerick lace began in 1883 when Mrs Vere O'Brien opened her first school. The story is best told in her own words:

> I went to live in Ireland in 1883 and was baffled by the difficulty of procuring the necessary materials, only the coarser kinds of net and thread being now supplied to the workers. I was helped over this difficulty by my husband's aunt, Lady de Vere, of Curragh Chase, Adare, herself a connoisseur in lace — who had some fine Brussels net and threads, with which I persuaded one of the older workers to make an experimental flounce from a design given me by our neighbour, the late Madam O'Grady, a born artist to her finger tips, and interested in every kind of handicraft. This first specimen of new old Limerick lace being a success, I invested in more fine net and thread, collected a few designs, chiefly from 'rubbings' of old Brussels or Point d'Alencon laces lent me by friends, and employed two or three more old workers — ex-factory hands — to make lace for me at their own homes. The 'market' for the revived lace was at first a very limited one, consisting chiefly of my husband, who helped me pay the workers, and then presented me with the lace produced by them, but soon friends came to our assistance, with private orders, and in time I had the pride and satisfaction of working for 'the trade', amongst our best employers in these early days being the late Mr Ben Lindsay, of Grafton Street, and Mr Biddle of Oxford Street, whose advice and criticism have all along been of the greatest service to me and my workers.[9]

Mrs Vere O'Brien's observations in relation to the revival of Limerick lace are modest; no one will question the statement that her efforts ensured its continuance. She excelled as designer, that most essential aspect of lacecraft, and as teacher. Her work supplemented and gave support to the sisters of the Convent of the Good Shepherd who remain the custodians of the Limerick school.

This ecclesiastical connection provided another outlet for Limerick lace — the making of lace-decorated surplices and albs for the clergy. But

Mrs Meredith in the 1860s had hinted at the coming challenge of crochet lace to the established schools.

Carrickmacross and Limerick lace were popular and sought after before the Famine of 1847. Of the many laces which developed after it two demand especial attention — Irish Point and Irish Crochet. Irish Point, a true lace (that is, a product of needle and thread) was introduced by the Presentation Sisters at their convent in Youghal. Exquisite in its design and fineness of execution, Youghal lace quite rightfully claims the title of 'Queen of Irish laces'. It owes its origin to a member of the community, Mother Mary Ann Smith, who, with ingenuity and patience, analysed a piece of Italian needlepoint and discovered the manner of its making. She encouraged her teachers to experiment and together they invented new stitches so that some specimens they made had twenty-five varieties.

In 1852 a lace-school was organised in the Youghal convent. The sisters of the community created the designs and the excellence of the final articles ensured that many prizes and awards were given to the school. The patrons of Youghal lace have included members of many royal families, ecclesiastical vestments were prepared for the hierarchy, and the presentation from the Bishops of Ireland of a rochet and altar piece to Leo XIII on the occasion of his jubilee gained a gold medal at the Vatican Exhibition in 1870. This flourishing industry made an important contribution to the lives of the poor in the severe depression of post-Famine years, and the prestige of the lace gained it many followers in other convents throughout the country.

Irish crochet was the second 'lace' introduced after the Famine. It had been known here before but it is in the post-Famine years that its great diffusion took place, and the centre of that diffusion was again a convent, this time the Ursuline Convent in Blackrock in County Cork. From Cork the art of crochet spread throughout the south, and again the making went far to alleviate the misery of the times. Mrs Meredith founded the Adelaide Crochet School in Cork, and her philanthropic activity was praised by a Mr Maguire in *The Irish Industrial Movement:*

> Of the many schools which have been brought under my observation, I do not know any one which presents more interesting features than the Adelaide School. At its first commencement it differed in no way from the ordinary industrial school, in which young persons are employed during the day; but since then its whole character has changed, and it may now be described as a central depot for the reception of work and the transaction of business. It employs young persons of limited means, or reduced circumstances, who are now but too happy to apply their talents to a useful and practical purpose, and in most instances with the purest of human motives — the wish to confer even modest comforts on relations who have fallen victims to the great calamity of this country.[10]

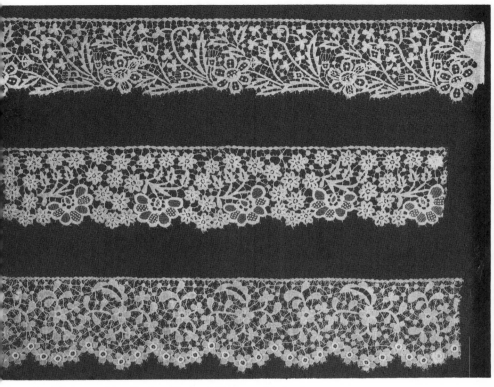

Carrickmacross Lace Borders, National Museum of Ireland

Mrs Meredith herself was critical of the low standard of much of this Cork crochet; her priorities were artistic as well as commercial. And her sense was that to satisfy commercial demand shoddiness of work was tolerated. Still, the enterprise had its success and went some way to relieve the distress of the poor. Mrs Meredith's efforts in the south were paralleled in the north under the patronage of Mrs Hand, wife of the Rector of Clones in County Monaghan. Here the success was both commercial and artistic and it is to Clones lace that the complimentary description 'Point d'Irlande' was applied.[11] At the century's end the encouragement given to lacemaking by religious communities, such as the Ursulines, and by private patrons such as Mrs Meredith and Mrs Hand, was supplemented by that of the Congested Districts Board whose sphere of operation was the poorest parts of the country. At this point we can leave the outline of the history of Irish lace to the end of the nineteenth century and turn to brief inspection of its varied techniques.

Our two older laces, Carrickmacross and Limerick, are not, in strict accuracy, lace, that is, a product solely of needle and thread. Both embellish an existing material. There are, however, distinctions to be drawn between them.

Carrickmacross lace is of two kinds, *appliqué* and *guipure*. *Appliqué* results from the following process. A design is prepared on stiff paper. This is then covered with machine-made net, and the net covered with fine muslin, all three being attached together. Using close sewing stitches the pattern is traced through the net and muslin. The design-paper is now removed, and the muslin cut away from the outline. The work now proceeds with fancy stitches on the net ground. *Guipure* is worked simply on a piece of close textured muslin on which the design has been drawn. When the design has been 'corded' (that is, outlined with thread), the centres are removed and the resulting spaces filled with open stitches and wheels, and buttonhole bars. Sometimes the two kinds were used in the one piece. The immediate influence on Carrickmacross *appliqué* is the *appliqué* produced in Brussels.

There are also two varieties of Limerick lace, *run* and *tambour*. In *run* lace the pattern is embroidered with a darning or running stitch on machine-made net. In *tambour* lace the design is embroidered on the net with a tambour hook (very similar to a crochet hook) using chain stitches. The two varieties were often combined in the one design.

Irish point is a true lace, produced entirely by the needle. It is a lace of great beauty requiring patience, skill and imagination. And so, finally, to *Irish crochet*. In origin it derives from attempts to imitate Italian needlepoint using a very fine crochet hook and cotton thread, but it soon developed its own characteristic motifs, and of all crochet lace it is the only one which achieved real distinction in design and execution. Most familiar, perhaps, is the variety worked from a central rose or sham-rock outwards to a square up to two inches in size, the squares being later joined invisibly to create the total design. The motifs of the single and double rose and the crown were elaborated in designs both intricate and artistic.

The story of Irish lace in the twentieth century is one of relative obscurity. Two factors, one historical, the other economic, are relevant. The improved economic situation led to the greater availability of alter-native sources of employment for working-class girls. The jam factory supplanted the lace-school. Some exploitation of the workforce attended the great post-Famine expansion. Lacemaking, essentially a rural phenomenon, had to yield when the economic environment became industrial. There was more dignity, too, in earning one's living where a choice was possible than in being the object of patronage, whether aristo-cratic or religious, no matter how enlightened that patronage was. Histor-ically, 'the stigma of poverty' attached itself to lacemaking, a stigma of course, not present in the upper classes of society where, as the Countess of Mayo observed in 1897, the lace-frame was a lady's 'close and intimate companion and elaborate art pieces filled the long hours of solitude'.

Also contributing to the decline was the falling off in the teaching of needlework in National Schools. And the lack of new designs led to

Detail of Carrickmacross Skirt Panel, National Museum of Ireland

repetition and debasement of earlier ones. While it is unlikely that Irish lacemaking will ever attain its earlier popularity, there are encouraging signs of interest and enthusiasm for it. Teachers throughout the country continue to inspire their pupils, demonstrating the satisfaction to be gained from making something of beauty. The Irish Countrywomen's Association has also been a staunch encourager and promoter and the Royal Dublin Society has continued to offer prizes and awards. The reward is now a personal one. Further, the cherishing of the tradition is in the skilled hands of the convents where so much of it originated. The founding of 'The Guild of Irish Lacemakers' was prompted by the desire to provide a forum for the exchange of ideas, and mutual encouragement as inheritors of an art of which our country is so deservedly proud.

Notes

1 George Pellew, *In Castle and Cabin or Talks in Ireland in 1887*, New York, 1888, 56.
2 Louisa Meredith, *The Lacemakers: Sketches of Irish Character*, London, 1965, p. vii.
3 'Fit for a Queen', RTE talk, 29 November 1980.
4 Meredith, pp. 5-6.
5 I am indebted here to Ada K. Longfield's *Guide to the Collection of Lace*. This *Guide* and the exhaustive research of Elizabeth Boyle, published in her *The Irish Flowers* (1971), have together added enormously to our knowledge of the history of Irish lace.
6 Mrs Robert Vere O'Brien, 'The Limerick Lace Industry', *The Irish Homestead*, 1897, p.24.
7 Elizabeth Boyle, *The Irish Flowers*, 1971, p.28.
8 Vere O'Brien, p 24.
9 *Ibid.*, 24-5.
10 Meredith, 12.
11 Technically, of course, Clones and other regional developments (more familiarly known as 'Irish Crochet') are not true laces.

Women Artists

Paula McCarthy

In the development of the visual arts in Ireland in this century, women appear prominently in two contexts. As artists, they introduced new styles and perfected older ones, playing an important role in the dynamic ferment of artistic progress. As the initiators and organisers of groups and societies, they contributed substantially also, making possible creative activity by others. Individuals figure in both contexts, and many count among the pioneers of the Irish arts today.

The women artists who emerged at the end of the nineteenth and the beginning of the twentieth centuries tended to come from upper-class families. They continued a tradition of travelling to Europe to complete their artistic training. In their personalities they were highly independent, and many remained unmarried. The history of their activities has as background the resurgence of national feeling throughout Ireland in the 1890s. The accompanying cultural revival led to the foundation of such organisations as the National Literary Society, the Gaelic League and the Gaelic Athletic Association. The groundwork was laid at this time for the growth and development of many visual arts institutions. Sarah Purser, for example, is important not only for her original works but for her involvement in the foundation of the Municipal Gallery of Modern Art, and for setting up her stained glass studio in which younger artists were trained in this medium.

Sarah Purser (1843—1943) was an accomplished portrait painter who studied at the Metropolitan School of Art in Dublin and at the Académie Julien in Paris. Of particular note are her early works, such as 'Lady Holding a Rattle' in which she demonstrates a light vivacious brushwork and an excellent sense of colour accented by rhythms of light and shade. However, a recent commentator has said: 'For Irish twentieth-century painting, the life of Sarah Purser is more important for the influence she had as a patron, a hostess, a collector and for her foundation of An Túr Gloine (The Tower of Glass) than for her paintings.'[1]

In late October 1901 she organised an exhibition of the works of John Butler Yeats and Nathaniel Hone, one outcome of which was the introduction of Hugh Lane to contemporary Irish art. He had just launched his own career as a highly successful dealer in London, and was in Ireland on a visit to his aunt, Lady Gregory. Influenced by Sarah Purser, in 1902—3 he mounted a winter exhibition of old masters in Ireland to assist the ailing Royal Hibernian Academy. Later, he put on an exhibition of Irish art in London. The Dublin Municipal Gallery opened in 1908 in temporary premises at Clonmel House in Harcourt Street, and Lane lent it a collection of paintings. He offered them as an outright gift on condition that a permanent gallery be provided. Lane's death on the 'Lusitania' in 1915 began a controversy about the disposal of the thirty-nine paintings, mostly by French Impressionists. He had grown so impatient with Dublin Corporation's delay in building a gallery that in 1913 he had bequeathed them to the National Gallery in London. Just before his departure to America in 1915, however, he added a codicil to his will, leaving them to Dublin. The codicil, signed but not witnessed, was invalid in law.

After Lane's death, Lady Gregory began a campaign to have the paintings returned to Ireland. On 14 February 1924 Sarah Purser founded the Friends of the National Collections of Ireland whose main purpose was to secure the return of Lane's gift to Dublin. A solution was not found until 1979, when it was agreed that the pictures should be divided into two groups, which are lent alternately to Dublin. The Friends remain in operation today and have made donations of works of art to museums throughout Ireland. It was Sarah Purser too who finally provided a solution to the problem of a permanent home for the proposed gallery of modern art for Dublin. She proposed to President Cosgrave that Charlemont House, which had just been vacated by the Department of the Registrar General, be used. This proposal was formally adopted by the government in February, 1929, and the Municipal Gallery of Modern Art opened in 1933.

In 1903, at the prompting of Edward Martyn, Sarah Purser founded An Túr Gloine, the stained glass studio where almost every well-known Irish artist was trained, and where Evie Hone and Wilhelmina Geddes worked. Though Sarah Purser designed a few windows, she almost never executed any; however, many windows originating from An Túr can be seen in Ireland today.

At the turn of the twentieth century an arts and crafts movement began whose patrons and contributors were predominantly women. An Arts and Crafts Society was founded in 1894 with the aim of fostering artistic industries in Ireland and promoting Irish culture, by means of lectures and exhibitions of Irish arts and crafts. Because the standard was low the first exhibitions, held in 1896 and 1899, were not very influential, but a third, held in 1904, was a great success. The change was largely due to the foundation of An Túr Gloine and the Dun Emer Guild; a reinforcement came from the fact that the Catholic Church had begun to direct commissions towards Irish artists.

The Dun Emer Guild was founded in 1902 by Evelyn Gleeson together with Elizabeth and Lily Yeats, daughters of John Butler Yeats and sisters of W. B. and Jack B. Yeats. The Guild specialised in embroidery, printing and tapestry making. By 1904 their enterprise split into two parts: the Dun Emer Guild continued under the direction of Evelyn

Hoey's Court, by Estella F. Solomons, etching (Courtesy Arts Council of Ireland)

Gleeson producing tapestries and woven carpets, and the Dun Emer
Industries, directed by the. Yeats sisters, engaged in embroidery, printing
and bookbinding. The Dun Emer Industries eventually became the Cuala

Industries, of which a subsidiary was the Cuala Press, which published books and illustrated broadsides of poetry by W. B. Yeats and others.

The career of Estella Solomons (1882-1968) shows less involvement with artistic groups but is touched by the political history of Ireland in the early twentieth century. She was the second of four children of a Dublin Jewish family. Her mother was accomplished in languages and music, and she received the usual education of a privileged young woman of the time, in Dublin and in Germany. She studied at the Metropolitan School of Art, alongside woman artists who would leave a mark on Irish art of the twentieth century; they included Eva Hamilton, Beatrice Elvery and Mary Swanzy. Her teachers, William Orpen and Walter Osborne, influenced her work: Orpen particularly her portraiture, while her sense of atmosphere and light and shade was derived from Osborne's work.

After some time in London at the Chelsea School of Art, and later in Paris, she came under the influence of Rembrandt. She visited a tercentenary exhibition of his work in Amsterdam in 1906 and studied in particular his use of light and shade to heighten dramatic effect. Her own finest work is her etchings, depicting Dublin scenes, dark alleyways, entrance-ways to pubs, women and children standing in doorways, or capturing the shadowy atmosphere, with light sifting through the windows, of the interior of Archbishop Marsh's Library.

Two younger women, whose careers form the basis of modern Irish art, were Mainie Jellett (1897–1944) and Evie Hone (1894–1955). Both came from prominent Anglo-Irish families; Mainie Jellett received her first painting lessons from Elizabeth Yeats. She first met her life-long friend and fellow-worker, Evie Hone, when she was twenty and studying under Walter Sickert at the Westminster Technical Institute in London. Together they travelled to Paris in 1921 to study at the Academy of André Lhote, where they learned the fundamentals of cubism.

In an essay, 'Definition of My Art', written in 1943, Mainie Jellett wrote:

> With Lhote I learned to use natural forms as a starting point towards the creation of form for its own sake; to use colour with the knowledge of its great potential force, and to produce work based on a knowledge of rhythmical form and organic colour, groping towards a conception of a picture being a creative organic whole but still based on a realistic form. I worked on these lines and developed a great deal but felt I had not gone as far as I wanted on the way to the full understanding of extreme forms of non-representational art.

Just then, Albert Gleizes had returned to Paris from New York, where his work had been acclaimed. While there, he had founded an exhibition entitled 'Independent Show' with Picabia and Marcel Duchamp. In 'Homage to Mainie Jellett' he writes: 'It was 1921. I was far from

Alice Milligan, by Estella F. Solomons, Ulster Museum

teaching anyone other than myself. The first manifestations of Cubism were already ten years old.'[2] Gleizes was now at the point where he was about to eliminate the subject totally from his canvas. He describes how Jellett and Hone came to his studio and insisted on working under his guidance.

They began working together every day and experimented in painting without subject. The initial period was difficult as Gleizes sought to articulate his ideas. As time progressed, however, the task became easier; Gleizes continues:

In 1922 I wrote 'Peinture et ses Lois, Ce Qui Devait Sortir du Cubisme', an imperfect study in many ways and certainly incomplete, but nevertheless, in its general structure and outline incontrovertible. I owe it to Mainie Jellett and Evie Hone and even today my feeling of gratitude shows no signs of leaving me.[3]

Mainie Jellett and Evie Hone returned to Paris every year until 1930 to work with Gleizes. By elminating the primacy of subject from the canvas, they experimented with form and colour to create spatial relationships. Their use of colour was dynamic and the forms were juxtaposed to create movement and depth within the picture plane.

Abstract, by Mainie Jellet (Courtesy Arts Council of Ireland)

In 1924 they held their first joint exhibition in Dublin. The critics reacted with disbelief and hostility, but the two artists remained undaunted. As they developed, their activities diverged: Jellett continuing to work in oil and watercolour, Hone turning, from the 1920s onwards, to stained glass. From 1933 she worked at An Túr Gloine, and became one of the country's most prominent and successful religious artists, executing commissions abroad as well as in Ireland. The most famous is the Eton College chapel window carried out between 1948 and 1952. Her style developed, displaying at first the influence of Cubism, later that of Rouault, and in the final phase becoming more bold and complex.

Meanwhile, Mainie Jellett combined with the practice of painting the roles of teacher, critic and protagonist of stylistic change. She made broadcasts on art on Radio Éireann, lectured and published essays. She had a clear vision of the artist's role in society: instead of being a recluse, the artist should, through creativity, be a contributor to all aspects of society. In 1943, a year before her death from cancer, she was one of the founders of the Irish Exhibition of Living Art, designed to provide a forum for the most avant-garde aspects of modern art. Their annual exhibition still provides that forum today.

Despite Mainie Jellett's enormous influence, Cubism was never fully accepted in Ireland. Artists who were influenced such as Mary Swanzy (1882—1979) and May Guinness (1863—1955) went on to develop their own personal styles. Grace Henry (1868—1953) remained totally unaffected, though she had studied under André Lhote in Paris.

The generation of artists who succeeded Hone and Jellett was subjected to the impact of Ireland's isolation, political, cultural and, in the years of the Second World War, military. A distinctive style in art developed, which has been defined as a 'poetic genre', evasive and introspective, influenced by the Irish landscape and soft light. These qualities permeate the work of women artists such as Nano Reid and Camille Souter. But before discussing their paintings we shall consider Norah McGuinness, whose work forms a bridge between this style and the earlier one influenced by Cubism.

Norah McGuinness (1903—1980) was born in Derry, the daughter of a coal-merchant and ship-owner. She came to Dublin in 1921 to attend the Metropolitan School of Art, where she came under the influence of the stained glass artist Harry Clarke. In 1925 she married the poet Geoffrey Phibbs, known as Geoffrey Taylor, and soon became involved in the exciting literary and theatrical world of Dublin in the 1920s. She designed sets for numerous plays, including Yeats's *The Only Jealousy of Emer* and *Deirdre*, and Georg Kaiser's *From Morn to Midnight*, for which she received admiring reviews in the *New Statesman*. The fine quality of her book illustrations led Yeats to ask her to provide drawings for *Stories of Red Hanrahan* and *The Secret Rose*.

In 1929 her marriage broke up and she decided to study in Paris. On the advice of Mainie Jellett she worked under Lhote. Her style changed

Bird, Sand and Sun by Norah McGuinness, oil on canvas, Bank of Ireland, College Green

significantly after two years with him, colour becoming more important, but she never became an abstract painter. Instead she turned almost exclusively to landscape painting, which was to be the predominant concern of Irish painters throughout the 1940s and 1950s.

From Paris she went on to London, and then in 1937 to America, where her work was shown, together with that of Jack B. Yeats, Nathaniel Hone and Nano Reid, in an Irish group exhibition. In 1944 she succeeded Mainie Jellett as president of the Irish Exhibition of Living Art. She held the position until 1970, when she and the entire committee resigned voluntarily in order to make way for a younger group of artists, an action indicating her broadmindedness and vision and her dislike of the idea of becoming part of an academic 'establishment'.

In her paintings she is primarily concerned with colour and the simplification of forms. She uses blocks of colour to create decorative patterns, and line to emphasise contours in the landscape. Figures rarely appear in her work, but when they do they are sharply outlined. There is also a highly personal use of space, where background and foreground are differentiated by colour. At times linear perspective does not exist at all, the most important element being the pattern on the picture plane.

The same preoccupation with landscape appears in the work of Nano Reid (1905–82), though she also painted portraits. Sean O'Faolain describes her thus:

Untitled, by Nano Reid;
drawing of a woman (photograph, Nano Reid Estate courtesy Arts Council of Ireland)

. . . poetic visionary, writing in code about things behind the seen surface, an imagination nurtured in the Boyne Valley whose rich uplands and ancient stones silently murmur ancestral memories . . . She never describes, she indicates, hints, suggests, but once we get the hang of her private code she is just as lucid as painters who speak openly through things made recognisable at a glance.

Thomas McGreevy, writing in *The Irish Times* in 1942, mentioned other aspects of her work:

> . . . her varied richness of invention, especially in the matter of colour, is balanced by an unusual economy in the means employed to express it. With a few strokes of her brush she can make boats at rest . . . seem funny and beautiful at once — a vivacious and touching poetry of effect which recalls the art of Raoul Dufy, though there is no trace of any debt to the distinguished Frenchman; Miss Reid's work is more solid than his.

Nano Reid was born in Drogheda and won a scholarship to the Metropolitan School of Art. In Dublin, like Norah McGuinness, she was influenced by Harry Clarke. She went to Paris in 1927 but spent only nine months there and did not study under any one master, which she later regretted. This was followed by a period in London, where she studied under Bernard Meninsky, and she returned to Dublin in 1930. In 1934, the year of her first one-woman show at The Gallery, Stephen's Green, she came under the influence of the Belgian painter Marie Howet, in whose work, according to Jeanne Sheehy, she saw the possibility of 'free and expressive use of paint'.

In the 1930s her work included portraits, done in a style full of strength and personality, which some sitters found unflattering; one asked for his money back. After this she did less portraiture, though she continued to paint her friends, and began to concentrate on landscape painting. With Norah McGuinness, she represented Ireland at the Venice Biennale of 1950.

Nano Reid chose to depict themes which were close to her. Her paintings have titles like 'Backyard', 'Tinkers at Slieve Breagh' or 'Ballads at the Bar'. Water frequently appears as a motif and Celtic subjects were inspired by the numerous Boyne Valley archaeological sites near her home. Studied closely, her paintings reveal a richness of images and a wonderfully dramatic use of colour.

A younger artist, Camille Souter (b. 1929) also paints in a personal style with its own quiet strength. She was born in England but was brought to Ireland shortly after her birth. She trained as a nurse and is self-taught as an artist. Her paintings have a strong element of abstraction, though she does not see a sharp distinction between abstract and realist painting. She displays the beauty of the most commonplace objects, such as fish or pieces of meat, transforming them by her feeling for light and texture. Recently she has discovered the same excitement in painting pictures of aeroplanes.

Maria Simmonds-Gooding (b. 1939) also shows a concern for landscape and for poetic values which may be compared with that found in the work of Reid and Souter. But Simmonds-Gooding is a strong individualist as well. Her work shows a preference for recording shapes in the countryside and she uses virtually no colour so as not to interfere with

Galway Peasant, by Nano Reid, Ulster Museum

Pair of Heads, by Hilary Heron (Estate of David Greene)

this objective.

There is a strong tendency for Irish art to remain essentially rural. Frances Ruane comments:

Artists are more likely to adapt the irregular organic shapes of the hillside than the geometry of machine parts. Hard-edged painting, pop imagery, computer art and dayglo colours originated in a 'hip' urban setting. International art has a calculated precision nurtured in a machine-dominated environment.[4]

While Irish artists in many cases resisted the impact of the hard-edged international style, the later 1960s saw the arrival of a new openness to outside influences, a wish to create an art expressive of urban experience. One event which may be read as a symptom of the new trend was the foundation of the international exhibition, 'Rosc', first held in 1967. But it is a trend that so far is more visible in the work of male artists than in that of women.

The work of Anne Madden does show some international influence. She combined hard-edge and colour field painting with a poetic interpretation of landscape. Born in London in 1932, she lived in the west of Ireland from 1945 to 1958, when she married the artist, Louis Le Brocquy, and moved to France. Such paintings as 'Great Outcrop' and 'Land Formation — The Burren' show a combination of hardness and softness; there is pure abstraction and yet there is a haunting realism in her attempts to capture the essence of the land. Dorothy Walker points out that:

> She was one of the first Irish artists to make use of diptychs or triptychs to fuse several distinct images into a coherent whole: the structure of these divisions acts as a steadying geometry on her natural fluidity. The evidence of Irish pre-history that is still visible in the landscape has also been of profound influence.

It is true also that her paintings have a massiveness which is generally the aim of the sculptor.

Nineteenth-century Ireland possesed a strong sculptural tradition, continuing into the twentieth century with the appearance of several highly talented artists in Dublin, including Oliver Sheppard, Andrew O'Connor, Albert Power and Jerome Connor. Sculpture in the 1950s and 1960s is distinguished by the emergence of a number of excellent women sculptors.

Hilary Heron (1923—77) worked in wood at the beginning of her career, later experimenting with other media. Her work has a tremendous strength and simplicity. One of the best known pieces, 'Crazy Jane', executed in welded steel, depicts a head with sharply jagged pieces of metal representing hair, placed on an undefined narrow body. The simplistic face resembles an African mask. Beneath the skilful handling of movement and spatial relationships we catch a glimpse of a keen sense of humour.

Her younger contemporary, Gerda Frömel, was born in 1931 in Schonberg, Czechoslovakia, and studied at schools in Stuttgart, Darmstadt and Munich. In 1956 she came to Ireland and spent a year in Dublin before returning to Munich. After her marriage to the sculptor and opera singer Werner Schurmann in 1965 she came to live in Ireland permanently.

Her work shows a strong Italian influence, particularly evident in her use of marble and alabaster. Her interest in Giacometti's work can be clearly seen in her long, sinuous bronze figures. Using alabaster and marble, she executed heads which seemed almost Celtic in their design. She also worked in aluminium and stainless steel. In her best-known sculpture, a large abstract work in stainless steel, commissioned by Carroll's of Dundalk, she positions three high narrow beams vertically in the centre of an artificial lake in front of the factory. The clustered beams seem to tower above the factory, as they move in the wind and cast reflections in the lake. Gerda Frömel died in 1974 in a drowning accident.

Deborah Brown, the Northern Irish sculptor, was born in 1927 and studied at the National College of Art and Design in Dublin before going to Paris. At first her style was representational, but in 1958 she came in contact with American abstract painting and became, ultimately, a purely abstract painter and sculptor. She began to add papier mâché to canvas to give her works a more three-dimensional quality; she moved on to fibreglass, which permitted her even greater creativity than before, both because of its plastic qualities and because of its transparency, which creates dramatic light-effects on the surface of her work. Many of her pieces remain untitled.

Alexandra Wejchert, a Polish artist who has made Ireland her home, is both sculptor and painter. Born in Cracow, she studied at the Warsaw Academy of Fine Arts. Her work includes reliefs, in which movement is created in many instances by using short pegs of different lengths, painted different colours, or different hues of one colour. Occasionally she resorts to rounded shapes or semi-circles which project at various angles from the surface. A build-up of these reliefs creates a striking effect of light and dark as shadows are cast in different directions. She has also worked with pure three-dimensional forms, making sculptures from coloured perspex, and here again the same undulating shapes occur.

The late 1960s and early 1970s saw an interesting development in the emergence of art history as a 'real' subject in third-level education. It is perhaps noteworthy that until very recently the heads of department in the subject of the two Dublin universities were women. The late Dr Françoise Henry taught at University College until 1973, and Professor Anne Crookshank heads the Department of History of Art at Trinity College, Dublin. Both these women have been responsible for the training of art historians, critics and arts administrators who are working in Ireland today.

Shortage of space makes it impossible to do more than name a few of the artists who have emerged during the 1970s and at the beginning of the 1980s, and who have added new dimensions to painting, sculpture,

Sculpture in Stainless Steel, by Gerda Frömel, Carroll's, Dundalk

graphics, performance and video art. Artists such as Eilis O'Connell, Aileen MacKeogh, Vivienne Roche and Alanna O'Kelly are contributing new ideas in sculpture and conceptual art; while Eithne Jordan and Cecily Brennan are emergent painters. The Graphic Studio has attracted many women artists, and fine graphics have been produced by artists such as Mary Farl Powers. The accomplishment of women remains an integral part of the achievement and history of the visual arts in Ireland.

Notes

1   Anne Crookshank and The Knight of Glin, *The Painters of Ireland, c. 1660-1920*. London 1978, 265.
2   Albert Gleizes, 'Homage to Mainie Jellett' in Eileen MacCarvill, ed. *Mainie Jellett: The Artist's Vision*, Dundalk 1958, 40-1.
3   *Ibid*.
4   Frances Ruane, Introduction to 'The Delighted Eye', an exhibition selected by Dr Frances Ruane as part of the festival, 'A Sense of Ireland', London 1980.

Further reading

Bruce Arnold, *A concise History of Irish Art*. New York, Washington 1968. *Mainie Jellett: 1897-1944*
Thomas Bodkin, *Hugh Lane and his Pictures*, Dublin, 1932.
Bank of Ireland, *Catalogue of Works*, Introduction by Anne Crookshank, Biographical Notes by Dorothy Walker.
Mike Catto, *Art in Ulster 2*, Belfast, 1977.
Anne Crookshank and The Knight of Glin, *The Painters of Ireland*, London, 1978.
Lady Gregory, *Case for the Return of Sir Hugh Lane's Pictures to Dublin*, Dublin, 1926.
Peter Harbison, Homan Potterton and Jeanne Sheehy, *Irish Art and Architecture*, London, 1978.
 Irish Art 1900-1950 (Text by Hilary Pyle) Cork 1975
 Irish Directions (Circulating Exhibition) Foreword by Dorothea Weedan and Alan Warhurst, Introduction by Ethna Waldron, 1974.
 The Irish Imagination 1959-1971 (Introduction by Brian O'Doherty) Catalogue in association with Rosc. 1971.
Michael Morrow, *Gerda Frömel — An Appreciation, Introspect* 1 (Dec. 1975), p. 20.
Jeanne Sheehy and George Mott *The Rediscovery of Ireland's Past*
 The Celtic Revival 1830-1930, London 1980.
Frances Ruane, *The Delighted Eye*, Belfast & Dublin, 1980.

Women as Writers: Dánta Grá to Maria Edgeworth

Eiléan Ní Chuilleanáin

The emergence of a significant number of women writers is a European phenomenon dating from the seventeenth century. In part, it can be explained as a facet of the emergence of the writer from the frequent anonymity of the middle ages, with greater value accorded by the Renaissance to the individual, including the feminine, person. Other Renaissance developments such as the invention of printing and the wide dissemination of fairly cheap books in the modern languages were also important: women writers appear, but so do women readers. Women's identification as a recognisable segment of the audience for literary works leads to a more acute examination than had previously been possible of their problems and their roles, an examination most effectively undertaken by writers who were women themselves.

In the early modern period literacy was limited and books relatively expensive; the weight of literary tradition was on the side of aristocratic subjects (especially in Ireland) and the reinforcement of existing social rules. We must expect, therefore, to find a bias towards the tastes and attitudes of the upper class. This restriction may be compensated for by the greater freedom enjoyed by upper-class women, the fact that they alone of their sex had experience of power, leisure, education and responsibility.

My intention is to look at changes in the literary milieu in Europe and Ireland, and to see how far national and international cultural change influenced works addressed to women, and more particularly works written by women in the period between the sixteenth and the early nineteenth century. The works I am dealing with include love-poetry, a famous poem of lamentation and some novels by the earliest good Irish novelist, Maria Edgeworth, one of whose main concerns was education. Thus we will also be looking at various stereotypes of women's roles: nurturing the new generation, bewailing the dead and focussing sexual images.

Traditionally, and most notably in such societies as Ireland's before 1601, the relationship between literature and society was often expressed as one between poet and patron. In other countries the patron might be a woman, but the well-defined political standing of the Irish poet meant that his primary patron had always by tradition been a man, the head of his nation. So if the poet addresses a woman, this is a secondary activity, not part of his main function. He may address a poem of praise to a chieftain and append a stanza of praise for the chieftain's wife as a post-script, naming her and detailing her ancestry, or he may express passionate and illicit love to an unnamed woman, but whether he expresses praise, gratitude, friendship or desire he speaks more or less in his private capacity.

The *Dánta Grá* of the period 1350—1750 (mostly thought to date from the latter half of this period) are the most distinguished productions of this secondary, private activity of the professional poets, alongside whom we find aristocratic amateurs. A few of these are women, so that in this context we may look for the earliest examples of Irish women as writers as well as considering the social and literary traditions governing the interactions of writers and readers.

Scholars from Robin Flower to Seán Ó Tuama have analysed the relationship of these Gaelic love-poems to the 'learned and fantastic' European tradition of courtly love dating back to twelfth-century Provence. There is plenty of disagreement among scholars about the origins and characteristics of this kind of poetry in Britain and on the continent; in Ireland the problem is complicated by anonymity, lack of certainty about dates and the wholesale destruction of manuscripts when the Gaelic aristocratic society collapsed. But the resemblances are evident; I would like to point instead to some deviations.

Love is often referred to in this tradition as a sickness, or a threat. The Gaelic poet is as aware as his continental model that the convention demands that he die for love, but a few striking poems affirm his determination to survive:

> O woman, shapely as the swan,
> On your account I shall not die!

So reads the best-known one, in Padraic Colum's translation. The poet's vigorous assertion of independence sets off the woman's assault with the weapons of her beauty; they emerge as equals locked in combat, rather than showing the European contrast between the lady's disdainful remoteness and the lover's despairing devotion. When a woman speaks in her own person one gets the same sense of a conflict of strong wills, or a possibility of their being united as a single will. Isabel Campbell, Countess of Argyll, writes:

> The love I gave in secret
> And must not betray
> If it can find no comfort
> My flower will decay

— accepting the notion of love as disease and suffering; but not as a suffering to be patiently borne. The poem ends:

> The man I gave my love to
> Whose name I can't say
> If he causes me trouble
> May he feel worst pain! [1]

In this kind of poetry we find women as metaphorical (killing with their beauty) or literal sexual aggressors; one of the most famous, *A bhean lán do stuaim*, is spoken by a man refusing a woman's advances. Women participate actively in the convention of love and love-poetry; a woman may be the recipient of a poem, or its author, within the narrow aristocratic world; or she may appear as critic. Bríd O'Donnell, born a Fitzgerald, comments in verse on a poem sent to her by an aristocratic lover, telling him that its professionalism has betrayed to her that not he but the bard O'Hussey is the real author. Both she and her lover, as amateurs, are capable of judging a virtuoso performance if not of equalling it. [2]

Besides the equality offered by sharing in an intimate, privileged world, there may be another reason for the confident self-expression of a poet like Isabel Campbell. Early Irish myth, as has been suggested elsewhere in this book, presents a series of powerful images of women: aggressive politically like Queen Maeve or erotically like Deirdre and Gráinne. But also, as Eleanor Knott remarks, of the 'small number of love-poems (that) have come down to us from the Old- and Middle-Irish period, (all) . . . are attributed to women'. [3] Such poems as the lament of Deirdre for the sons of Uisneach, or Liadain's on her love for Cuirthir, may be assigned to legendary characters, but in them we hear a feminine voice that is learnedly articulate as well as passionate. And they link the theme of love to the female tradition of lamentation which persisted in reality from legendary times until the present century.

Outside the cultivated, archaic world of poets, ladies and chieftains, the public world was, in culture and politics, rapidly changing from the sixteenth century on. All over Europe literature was detaching itself from aristocratic patronage and addressing itself to a wider audience, limited, it is true, by the realities of illiteracy and poverty, which put it out of the reach many. But among those with the money for books and the ability and leisure to read them, women of the middle and upper classes formed a significant proportion — a fact widely commented on at the time. In the sixteenth and seventeenth centuries they read romances, and as the romance gradually changes into the novel women appear themselves as original, professional creators of fictions addressed largely to their own kind. These reflected not only their interests as women but the concerns of the class to which they belonged.

The early modern novel is evidence for an increased vigour and a self-confidence of the vernacular languages of Europe, long unsure of themselves by comparison with the greater prestige of Latin and Greek. As women did not receive a classical education, their culture had always been rooted in the vernacular. They learned at home, not at school; and they taught in the home as well. Sir Thomas More, writing to Oxford University in 1518 on its duty of encouraging classical learning, declares that apart from this 'children can receive a good education at home from their mothers'. At the time when courts were reaching the end of their importance as centres of culture, ordinary dwellings were becoming more luxurious and offering more privacy. There was an increased respect for marriage and for the family as the place where moral values are instilled, and at the same time a greater respect for the ordinary speech of the family and the home.

As the Renaissance produced a new theory of human nature and a line of outstanding individuals who seem to illustrate the theory, it also asserted women's moral and intellectual equality with men. Castiglione's *Book of the Courtier*, for instance, quotes the standard arguments for women's inferiority and answers them: 'Everything men can understand, women can too; and where a man's intellect can penetrate, so along with it can a woman's . . . Women are naturally capable of the same virtues as men, and we have often seen the fruits of this.' But more importantly than mere defence or assertion, the literary works of the sixteenth century show a shift from the debate about whether the existence of women is a good or a bad thing to an examination of women's capacity for independent action, the nature and limitations of their freedom to be individuals. Such preoccupations can be found in unrealistic romance — for example in the many Renaissance works in which a girl disguises herself as a man and can then undertake adventures from which custom bars her sex, while reminding us, like Rosalind, that she 'has not a doublet and hose in her disposition'. *The Countess of Pembroke's Arcadia*, written by Sir Philip Sidney for his sister, has a heroine who is forced into taking independent action — consenting to run away with a lover — because of the folly, depravity and neglect of her parents. However fantastic the Arcadian setting, the problem she faces is that of the Jane Austen heroine, on whom autonomous, responsible action is often forced by circumstances, especially the circumstance of a stupid or irresponsible family.

The appearance of women as agents, with problems the author takes seriously, coincides with the lessening of the prestige of physical combat as a theme. War, says Milton, was 'hitherto the only argument/Heroic deemed'. Now it suddenly looked old-fashioned compared with moral struggle, 'the better fortitude'. All over Europe, aristocracies had lost their original military function and acquired a new function as public servants and a new interest in money. Literature belatedly reflects this change by mocking or moralising the old tales of brute force in which physical courage was the highest-prized virtue. The new literature consciously centres on moral dilemmas, shown in a more and more complex way as account is taken of contemporary social circumstances, often in a mock-heroic style, as in *Don Quixote*. The chivalrous knight makes way for the ideal country gentleman.

But in Ireland the traditional aristocracy was not changed but destroyed: exiled, pushed out by colonial land-grabbers or simply reduced in status. The loss of its primitive, military function which it had been exercising well into the seventeenth century led to the eclipse of native aristocracy itself. The vernacular, Gaelic, which throughout the Middle Ages had enjoyed the prestige of a learned language, began a decline in importance and a diminution of the area where it was spoken which has never been reversed. The Irish version of Quixote, the broken-down gentleman, becomes a feature of the Irish literary scene, fully recognisable by the time of Maria Edgeworth's *Castle Rackrent*.

In this crisis of cultural history, women may have continued as the guardians of vernacular culture, but their chance of contributing to the emergence of new literary forms as their English-speaking contemporaries did was slender. The novel was born of commerce, of metropolitan publishing houses and central distribution; the Gaelic world was relegated to the margins of culture. The most striking Gaelic work of the eighteenth century composed by a woman belongs to an archaic form and reflects a peculiar Irish custom, that of keening, much remarked on by travellers to Ireland until its near-disappearance in the present century. The custom is also found among many primitive peoples. The association of women with death which is at the centre of the keening custom is discussed elsewhere in this book. It might appear to belong among the most stultifying traditional views of women, associating them with passivity and surrender to natural forces, men with activity and life. The poem I am looking at, the *Caoineadh Áirt Uí Laoghaire*, tells another story, though.

Its author was Eibhlín Dubh Ní Chonaill, a member of the Derrynane family which in the next generation produced Daniel O'Connell the Liberator.[4] As her mother, Máire Ní Dhuibh, was a poet too, we can imagine a thriving feminine household culture at Derrynane; tradition suggests that the women had their imperious, independent natures in common, and the pride of class which Eibhlín expresses so forcefully may well come from the same source. Various members of the O'Connell family were educated on the continent; Eibhlín's husband, Art Ó Laoghaire, had been a colonel in the Austrian army, and her sister too married an Irishman in the Austrian service and emigrated — the empress Maria Theresa stood godmother to her eldest child. Both distance from the centre of English-speaking culture and administration and adverse discrimination which they suffered as Catholics made this Kerry family preserve its links with continental Europe; the international dimension of earlier Irish aristocratic culture was not lost.

Art Ó Laoghaire was Eibhlín's second husband and younger than herself. A quarrel between him and a Protestant neighbour, Morris, was embittered by his opponent's invoking the penal law empowering him to buy the best horse belonging to any Catholic for five pounds. (The intention of the law was to prevent the remnants of the Catholic upper class from ever threatening the English supremacy, a horse worth as much as five pounds being considered an engine of war — thus it is a blow to that class's conception of itself as an aristocracy, and it was a particular insult to Art as he had been a soldier.) Art refused to comply with the law; instead he went into hiding. Morris heard that Art had threatened his life, and applied for and got police protection. On 4 May 1773 Art Ó Laoghaire entered a public house at Carraig an Ime, about twenty miles from Millstreet, where Morris was staying, called for a drink of rum and let it be known in conversation that he intended to ambush his enemy on the road that night. Word was passed to the intended victim and it was Art who was taken by surprise and forced to retreat towards his home; at Carraig an Ime he was shot and the brown mare which had become the symbol of the conflict bolted for home. Eibhlín Dubh's poem tells how she reacted when she saw it:

> *Mo chara thu go daingean!*
> *Is níor chreideas riamh dod mharbh*
> *Gur tháinig chugham do chapall*
> *Is a srianta léi go talamh,*
> *Is fuil do chroí ar a leacain*
> *Siar go t'iallait ghreanta*
> *Mar a mbítheá id shuí 's id sheasamh.*
> *Thugas léim go tairsigh,*
> *An dara léim go geata,*
> *An tríú léim ar do chapall.*
>
> *Do bhuaileas go luath mo bhasa*
> *Is do bhaineas as na reathaibh*
> *Chomh maith is bhí sé agam,*
> *Go bhfuaireas romham tú marbh*
> *Cois toirín ísil aitinn,*
> *Gan Pápa gan easpag,*
> *Gan cléireach gan sagart*
> *Do léifeadh ort an tsailm,*
> *Ach seanbhean chríonna chaite*
> *Do leath orth binn dá fallaing —*
> *Do chuid fola leat 'na sraithibh;*
> *Is níor fhanas le hí ghlanadh*
> *Ach í ól suas lem bhasaibh.*   (ll 62—84)

> (My friend you were forever!
> I knew nothing of your murder
> Till your horse came to the stable
> With the reins beneath her trailing
> And your heart's blood on her shoulders
> Staining the tooled saddle

Where you used to sit and stand.
My first leap reached the threshold,
My second reached the gateway,
My third leap reached the saddle.

I struck my hands together
And I made the bay horse gallop
As fast as I was able,
Till I found you dead before me
Beside a little furze-bush
Without Pope or bishop,
Without priest or cleric
To read the death-psalms for you,
But a spent old woman only
Who spread her cloak to shroud you —
You heart's blood was still flowing;
I did not stay to wipe it
But filled my hands and drank it.)

This striking passage as well as conveying passion and grief shows us a woman whose image of herself emphasises action and movement. By contrast with the lone mourner who might be death personified, the *sean-bhean chrionna chaite* whom she finds attending on Art's body, she is all decisive vigour. It is her self-portrait that gives the poem its central life, though the *Caoineadh* contains several descriptions of her husband. There is the famous opening:

Mo ghrá go daingean tu!
Lá dá bhfaca thu
Ag ceann tí an mhargaidh,
Thug mo shúil aire dhuit,
Thug mo chroí taitneamh duit,
D'éalaíos óm charaid leat
I bhfad ó bhaile leat.   (ll 1—7)

(My love forever!
The day I first saw you
At the end of the market-house,
My eye observed you,
My heart approved you,
I fled from my friends with you,
Far from my home with you.)

From the start, she emphasises how she acts on her impulses. The rhythm of the lament is varied; one passage seems to answer another, in part because of the social nature of keening in which different speakers have their say from time to time. But the rhythm of responses can also suggest a relationship. The second section tells how she never regretted her elopement. Whereas at first Art is the direct object of her vision, the language as the poem develops makes use of more complex prepositional phrases, emphasised by repetition: 'You whitened parlours for me/ Reddened rooms for me'. Luxury develops into liberty: 'I could sleep in duck's feathers/Till midday milking-time/Or longer if I liked'.

She moves back to her memory of that first sight of him. It mostly suggests a dominant, even threatening figure, poised to assault an enemy, but it is introduced by a phrase in which he is passively *dressed* in his accoutrements, 'how well your hat suited you'. So the poem builds up a framework in which she and her lover/husband are alternately active and passive. The passivity of his dead, abandoned body is balanced by the picture of him alive, not merely as the mounted aristocrat but as the joking husband:

> *Nuair ghabhais amach an geata*
> *D'fhillis ar ais go tapaidh,*
> *Do phógais do dhís leanbh*
> *Do phógais mise ar bharra baise.*
> *Dúraís, 'A Eibhlín, éirigh id sheasamh*
> *Agus cuir do ghnó chun taisce*
> *Go luaimhneach is go tapaidh*
> *Táimse ag fágáil an bhaile,*
> *Is ní móide go deo go gcasfainn.'*
> *Níor dheineas dá chaint ach magadh,*
> *Mar bhíodh á rá liom go minic cheana.*   (II 168—78)

> (When you went out through the gateway
> You turned and came back quickly,
> You kissed your two children,
> You kissed me on the forehead.
> You said: 'Eileen, rise up quickly,
> Put your affairs in order
> With speed and with decision.
> I am leaving home now
> And there's no telling if I'll return.'
> I mocked this way of talking,
> He had said it to me so often.)

Here for once he speaks; he issues a command, but it is a call to action on her own account ('put *your* affairs in order') which she however doesn't take seriously as such. Again, she can take a snide reference by her sister-in-law to his popularity with women and transform it to a generous pride in his virility. Against the same sister-in-law she defends herself from the charge of having gone to bed on the night of the wake — the children were refusing to sleep unless she lay down with them. She presents herself as a person fully alive and responsible in all of her relationships, as lover, mother and as the avenger of her husband:

> *Tá fhios ag Íosa Críost*
> *Ná beidh caidhp ar bhathas mo chinn,*
> *Ná léine chnis lem thaoibh,*
> *Ná bróg ar thrácht mo bhoinn:*
> *Ná trioscán ar fuaid mo thí,*
> *Ná srian leis an láir ndoinn,*
> *Ná caithfidh mé le dlí,*
> *'S go raghad anonn thar toinn*
> *Ag comhrá leis an rí,*
> *'S mara gcuirfidh ionam aon tsuim*
> *Go dtiocfad ar ais arís*
> *Go bodach na fola duibhe*
> *A bhain díom féin mo mhaoin.*   (II 315–27)

(Jesus Christ knows
I'll have no cap on my head,
Nor a shift on my back,
Nor shoes on my feet,
Nor goods in my house,
Nor the brown mare's harness
That I won't spend on lawyers;
That I'll cross the seas
And talk to the king,
And if no one listens
That I'll come back
To the black-blooded clown
That took my treasure from me.)

The death of an individual, the decline of the native aristocracy, can only be countered by this affirmation which transforms the keen, from an instrument of communal acceptance of the inevitable, to an assertion of personal freedom. As with the women of the *Dánta Grá*, as also with those of early Irish legend, sexuality is a force related to the will. Paradoxically, the archaic situation and convention of the keen combine with the theme of love to liberate a legendary and aristocratic energy.

When Eibhlín Dubh vents her anger at the informer with the contemptuous question, 'If you wanted a bribe/Why didn't you come to me?/I'd have given you anything . . .' she proclaims her independence by relegating him to a lower class. His is moneygrubbing; hers is capable of a mythological generosity. She ranges herself on the side of the oral tradition which, though transmitted and preserved by the ordinary people, often (as in the Border Ballads) concerns itself with the striking deeds of upper-class heroes. The *Caoineadh*, apparently composed extempore and already fitted for survival in the popular memory by its use of repetition and formulae, was passed on to later generations by a keening woman named Norry Singleton, from whose recitation it was written down about thirty years after its composition. Its origin in a notorious public quarrel no doubt contributed to its reputation, especially as the memorable clash of individuals was also seen as a confrontation between ancient Gaelic family pride and low-born colonial intrusion.

If Eibhlín's is the voice of a class, it is also that of a party within that class. The historical situation in Ireland and the particular events she commemorates make this inevitable, as do the language she writes in and the convention of the *caoineadh* in which the dead man is necessarily praised unreservedly and his enemies vilified.

Comparing Eibhlín Dubh with a woman poet of the early nineteenth century, Máire Buí Ní Laoghaire, we can see that not only has the pride of ancient Gaelic culture been replaced by a ferocious but shallow loyalty to party and the Catholic Church; Máire Buí has a much more tenuous sense of herself than Eibhlín Dubh. She came from a lower social class which by the 1820s was suffering from the historical misfortunes that preceded the great Famine of the 1840s. At her best, in *Cath Chéim an Fhiaidh*, her personality is quite submerged in the partisan triumph of the people whose deeds she celebrates. Elsewhere, she appears as a semi-anonymous figure, even referring to herself in masculine terms as we cannot imagine the earlier poet doing. As the Gaelic language and its speakers are assaulted by the disasters of the nineteenth century, a woman's right to speak in her own person may also be threatened.

One can imagine the tale of Art Ó Laoghaire's destruction as it might have been told by Maria Edgeworth, tragi-comically perhaps as in *Castle Rackrent* or in the moralising vein of her later work which often has affinities with tragedy, as she traces the connection between a single weakness or delusion and the individual's total downfall. The pride and recklessness of the Irish gentry, the vindictiveness of Morris and his likes, appear often enough in the books she wrote about Ireland. The novel form itself gives her the opportunity to maintain a kind of balance, to make a fine distinction between the absurd but noble and generous pride of King Corny in *Ormond* and the mere snobbery of the Clonbronys in *The Absentee*, and to set these off against the meanness of Protestant bigotry in Mrs McCrule (*Ormond*) or the treachery of the agent Garraghty (*The Absentee*).

In Edgeworth's Irish novels women appear often in roles that have little to do with the drama of sexual choice, traditionally the novel's main concern. They may be victims (like the Lady Rackrent who was locked in her room for her husband's lifetime), predators (like the later lady of the same name who opens a free school for the tenants' children where the children are forced to spend their time spinning flax for her) or objects of the hero's aspiration to be kept off-stage for the main part of the action and united with him at the end. The novel in which Maria Edgeworth most fully discusses female concerns, sexual and social, is *Belinda*, which is set in London. Party politics are mentioned in it, but they appear only as a form of dissipation or distraction. The main arena is the classic one, the family and the home.

As in other novels of the period, by Fanny Burney and Jane Austen for example, the heroine is a young girl who has been sent to a city to pick up a husband; brought up by a match-making aunt, whose main interest is in getting her 'established', she has been invited to stay in the London house of Lady Delacour. Jane Austen's young women sometimes have absent, more often inadequate parents; Fanny Burney's Evelina is thought to be illegitimate and so has in an acute sense no home. These characters are often successful in finding adequate parent-figures, older advisers who prevent their stories from ending tragically like Richardson's *Clarissa*. Lady Delacour, however, though a sympathetic character, is unable to adopt this role for Belinda, so that the heroine is doubly motherless and doubly homeless too, for Lady Delacour's house is so divided that it cannot, until it is reformed, be a home to anybody.

Lady Delacour's name suggests that the novel is planned to deal specifically with the problems of upper-class life; it was praised when it appeared for its accurate capturing of the tone of the best society. The problems of aristocratic life are doubly felt by women: leisure, education and freedom are given to them, not balanced by responsibility or power.

Discussions of women's education assume that they will have leisure: Maria Edgeworth writes elsewhere, 'neither the necessity of earning their bread, nor the ambition to shine in public affairs, hurry or prejudice their minds: in domestic life they have leisure to be wise'.[5] But education may lead to dissatisfaction with the restricted social role of women, and this discontent to an aping of masculinity which enslaves rather than liberates.

The history of Lady Delacour's life up to her friendship with Belinda illustrates an inability to evolve a genuine feminine freedom. Her marriage is a failure, symbolised by the existence in the house of separate staircases leading to the separate apartments of husband and wife — an architectural custom also condemned in *Ormond*. Her husband is given to the manly vices of gambling and drunkenness. Her children have been sacrificed to fashion, one born dead because the mother refused to rest during pregnancy, one dying because the mother insisted on feeding it herself in accordance with the sentimental fashion of the time. The third is rejected by the father because she is not a boy and kept at a distance by the mother who by now believes herself unfit to bring her up.

The failure to succeed in female bodily functions is dramatised by the major discovery Lady Delacour makes to Belinda: she believes she is dying of cancer of the breast. Again, she is guilty, not unlucky: the illness began when, at the height of her pseudo-masculinity, she set out to fight a duel with another woman, both dressed in men's clothes. The duel is ritually disposed of as both parties agree to fire in the air, but Lady Delacour's pistol recoils and strikes her on the breast.

The duel takes place as a result of a quarrel during an election; the two women have been campaigning on opposite sides, in spite of the fact that, of course, neither has a vote. The duel, like their canvassing, is an empty, imitative activity; Lady Delacour's opponent 'wished she were a man, that she might be qualified to take proper notice of my conduct';[6] Lady Delacour has a 'prodigious deference for the masculine superiority'[7] of the understanding of the (female) friend who talks her into issuing the challenge. Her opponent as well as duelling and canvassing is a gambler; but this too is a fake: she cheats at cards. A real duel has been fought already in the story; in it, Lord Delacour has killed the man wrongly thought to be his wife's lover, and she accepts the guilt for his death as she had foolishly encouraged him.

Freedom has reduced Lady Delacour to impotence; she cannot be wife, lover or mother — when she is embraced by her daughter she screams in agony. She needs to discover a different kind of freedom, which will be authentic, not imitative. Her experiences have put a distance between her and her female identity, which has been a source only of suffering and destruction to her. Outwardly her behaviour is founded on her sexual desirability; she is 'admired' by men whom she 'leads about'. But her breast, whose maternal function was such a failure, will destroy her unless it is removed (this at least is assumed for much of the novel — in fact it turns out that she has not got cancer). A good deal of the novel is taken up with the efforts of Belinda to persuade her to go to a good doctor and have the mastectomy operation if necessary, and with Lady Delacour's obsession with preserving the secret of her condition from the world, including her daughter and her husband. Her regeneration begins when she takes Belinda into her confidence, treating another woman as an autonomous being rather than an instrument. Hitherto she has shared her secret only with her maid and a quack doctor, both of whom she despises.

Secrecy, withdrawal and manipulation of others are her defence against a world where her assertion of freedom has proved valueless; neither she nor Belinda, however, can accept the conventional passivity of women, where they are praised for languor and indolence or regarded as commodities, their mental activities classified as 'accomplishments' which heighten their market value: 'Belinda Portman and her accomplishments, I'll swear, were as well advertised as Packwood's razor strops.'[8] But between the two extremes of frantic, imitative activity and the acceptance of passivity, there is not just the possibility but the absolute need of adequately motivated and resolved action on one's own behalf; the women characters are fighting for survival, against death in Lady Delacour's case but also against the eclipse of their personalities. Belinda is struggling to achieve respect in the humiliating world of the marriage-market, while Lady Delacour's daughter Helena, a child of 'ten or twelve' is fighting to gain her mother's love. The Amazons, frequently invoked by Lady Delacour in allusion to her threatened mastectomy, function as images of female courage and activity but are an inadequate image, superseded by the 'civil courage' which one character praises in terms reminiscent of Castiglione:

. . . military courage, that seeks the bubble reputation even in the cannon's mouth, may be had for sixpence a day. But civil courage, such as enabled the princess Parizade, in the Arabian Tales, to go straight up the hill to her object, though the magical multitude of advising and abusive voices continually called to her to turn back, is one of the rarest qualities in man or woman, and not to be had for love, money or admiration.[9]

The writer of novels in 1800 was faced with the same problems as her characters, the devising of action strong enough to be taken seriously and yet not violent or unrealistic. By making her subject the friendship between two women, and the problems one of them creates for another by burdening her with a secret of life and death, Maria Edgeworth avoids overloading her story with sexual motives — a subject that is never quite at the centre of her interest anyway. Both women, however, live in a world that is extremely interested in sex and equally with the consequence of sex, children. By showing us strong emotion and resolute action in the little girl, Helena, the novelist corrects Lady Delacour's half-acceptance of the grouping of women, children and idiots as unfit to act for themselves: 'I am neither a child nor a fool . . . consequently, there can be no pretence for *managing* me,'[10] she argues in defence of her resolution to have her operation performed by an unqualified practitioner and without telling her husband that she is ill. Helena's action — preventing a curious servant from opening the door of the secret room where Lady Delacour keeps her medicines — also has to do with proving oneself capable of respecting another's privacy. Belinda, older and less protected, also has to cope with the moral dilemma of her obligation to keep her friend's secret and her own reputation while attempting positively to promote her own and her friend's survival.

The philosophic Dr X is asked by Clarence Hervey, in love with Belinda, what he thinks of her; he replies, 'I must see Belinda act.'[11] The reader needs to do the same. The action which displays her virtue is occasionally melodramatically presented; the event that confirms Dr X's good opinion of her is her managing of Lord Delacour when he drunkenly attempts to enter the secret room while his wife is in convulsions brought on by a carriage accident. The problems created by drink, fast driving and lack of communication between husband and wife can be taken seriously by any age as both acute and likely, even if their presentation is occasionally awkward.

Belinda has been criticised on a number of grounds: the anticlimax of the discovery that Lady Delacour is not after all dying of cancer, and a long intrusive insertion suggested by Maria Edgeworth's father in which Belinda's lover, Clarence Hervey, is revealed to have a previous entanglement; like Richard Lovel Edgeworth's friend Day, the author of *Sandford and Merton*, he has set out to educate a girl brought up in complete seclusion as a wife for himself. The episode is out of character and ends rather farcically, but it does underline the novelist's theme of the importance of women having full access to the benefits of civilistion, as well as reinforcing her preoccupation with education generally and repeating the theme of reconciliation between fathers and daughters — the child of nature has a long-lost father who searches for her only after the son for whom he had planned a great future has died.

Lady Delacour's survival may indeed mar the tragic picture of the dying mother pretending indifference to her child in order to spare her suffering; but throughout the novel there are references to the possibilities of tragi-comedy as a genre outlawed by classical criticism of the stage but, by implication, permissible to the novelist. Lady Delacour and Belinda attend a ball, one dressed as the Muse of Tragedy, the other of Comedy; Lady Delacour insists that they change clothes secretly. On the same night she begins her confession of her secret and her history, and on the following day completes them. She speaks of 'folly which has brought on me all the punishments of guilt . . . (I have) nothing worse than folly to conceal: that's bad enough — for a woman who is known to play the fool is always suspected of playing the devil'.[12]

In classical theory, tragedy deals with guilt, comedy with folly, but Lady Delacour is pointing out that these concepts and their consequences are different for women and men. Survival for a woman is not eased by these conventions; she must invent her own genres, such as the developing one of the novel. More important, at every juncture in her life she must express herself in language that is complex, correct and if possible witty. If Lady Delacour can only be a melancholy warning to Belinda in the moral conduct of her life, at every turn she is a brilliant example of the critical approach to language. Schoolmistresslike, she raps her husband for his drunkenness and his bad grammar at once; she sees language as an important strategy in her own survival: 'What a nice grammarian a woman had need to be, who would live well with a husband inferior to her in understanding,'[13] she observes, after she has been reconciled to him. Her reconciliation to her daughter poses problems of secrecy. The little girl observes, 'I hope, mother, that you do not think I would try to find out any thing that you wish, or that I imagined you wished, I should not know.'[14] Challenged, she repeats the complex sentence in 'nearly the same words', thus forcing her mother to take her claim to trustworthiness seriously.

The concern with correct language and elegance of style which is evident throughout the book is not merely part of Maria Edgeworth's educational preoccupation. It is the style of speech, of social intercourse, that attracts her attention, not written style; and speech is important because it both reveals and conceals the private essence of character. Social convention and necessity may dictate concealment; a 'man of honour' will 'keep his mistress's secret'[15] — but there may in reality be no secret affair to hide, as emerges more than once in the book. A character articulates its anti-romantic tendency, its impatience with secrecy:

The struggles between duty and passion may be the charm of romance, but must be the misery of real life. The woman who . . . nourishes in secret a *fatal* prepossession for her first love, may perhaps, by the eloquence of a fine writer, be made an interesting heroine; — but would any man of sense or feeling choose to be troubled with such a wife? . . . Husbands may sometimes have delicate feeling as well as their wives, though they are seldom allowed to have any by these unjust novel writers.[16]

The protest against romance is in the name of *feeling* as well as sense; the assertion that not only women have feelings is the corollary of the one that not only men have brains. The triumph of the family at the end of the novel, in which both sexes can abandon their specialised frivolities, is an assertion of the possibilities of communication between men and women. The transformation of two irresponsible fathers, their acceptance of the sex of their daughters, does not only mirror the extremely important educational, emotional and co-operative relationship between Maria Edgeworth and her own father; it also provides a footnote to the conventional role-division by which all responsibility for the nurturing of the young devolved on the female. The question of upper-class leisure which began Lady Delacour's problems is solved for her husband as well as herself by the developing of their own talents (even he, it turns out, has some) and their daughter's.

Neither Maria Edgeworth nor Eibhlín Ni Chonaill wanted to revolu-ionise the position of women in European society. They both belonged, though each of them was untypical, to an international upper class, though not to the highest level of it, that had space for women like them. Their background and responsibilities, their international connections, were remarkably similar. Maria Edgeworth was throughout her writing life a widely known celebrity; Eibhlín Dubh's history and her poem rapidly became a part of the oral culture of her countryside. Their place in the established social framework of early modern Ireland enabled them to write with the same freedom and authority as the earlier women poets; as in the world of the *Dánta Grá*, their amateur status, their involvement with home and family and their restricted public enfran-chisement were not felt as disadvantages, but as part of the reality of life for their class.

A common element in the achievement of these writers — more pronounced in the Irish women than in Jane Austen or Fanny Burney, though recognisable too in a poet such as the seventeenth-century American Anne Bradstreet — is the presentation of their central female figures as engaged in warm, co-operative, often erotic but often, too, simply generous, relations with men. Behind this lies not only community of economic interest but a shared sense of style.

Notes

1 T.F. O'Rahilly (ed.), *Dánta Grádha*, 2nd ed., Dublin and Cork 1926, pp 74-5.
2 See Cathal Ó Háinle, *Promhadh Pinn*, Maynooth 1978, pp 22-3.
3 Eleanor Knott, *Irish Classical Poetry*, Mercier Press 1978, p 33.
4 For the story of the poem's composition, see the edition by Seán Ó Tuama (An Clóchomhar 1961, pp 7-31). All quotations are from this edition; the English versions are by Eilís Dillon. See also Mrs Morgan O'Connell, *The Last Colonel of the Irish Brigade*, London, 1892.
5 Maria Edgeworth, *Letter from a Gentleman to his Friend upon the Birth of a Daughter, with the Answer*, in *Leonora, with Letters on Several Subjects*, London, 1833, p 304.
6 Maria Edgeworth, *Belinda*, London 1833, Vol. I, p 70c.
7 *Belinda, loc. cit.*
8 *Ibid.*, Vol. I, p 28.
9 *Ibid.*, Vol. II, p 308; cf. Baldesar Castiglione, *The Book of the Courtier*, trans. George Bull, Penguin, 1976. p 223.
10 *Ibid.* Vol. I, p 248.
11 *Ibid.*, Vol. I, p 152.
12 *Ibid.*, Vol. I, pp 38, 43.
13 *Ibid.*, Vol. II, p 162.
14 *Ibid.*, Vol. II, p 81.
15 *Ibid.*, Vol. II, p 342.
16 *Ibid.*, Vol. II, pp 31-2.

Irish Women & Writing in Modern Ireland

Nuala O'Faolain

My title needs some explaining. Modern Ireland has many birth certificates, not all of them valid. In the history of literature periods are given beginning and ending dates, not necessarily those on the nation's birth certificates. Modern Ireland could be dated from the end of the 1840s' Famine, and the immediate relevance of that decade to writing would be the advance it marks in the primacy of the English language. From the point of view of a mass audience for print, modern Ireland begins with the establishment of literacy, again in English, around the same time. If, however, modern Ireland is a socio-economic characterisation, marked by peasant proprietorship, then the Land League, the Land Acts, and the philosophy — or cultural vision — of Éamon de Valera are the shaping events of what we are now, and modern Irish literature is both an element in and an expression of that sense of what we are now. But, what are we now? In small industrial estates, in ribbons of new bungalows, in the decor of a lounge bar, we can see that another Ireland superseded de Valera's, or, more accurately, has, since the 1950s, been superimposed upon his. We are now a neo-American, small-capitalist nation, whatever the rhetoric of our founding events.

It is not, of course, surprising that history offers no neat endings and beginnings. Not even the individual life does that, much less the collective. And yet academic decorum, most especially in the history of literature, pretends that we can tidy up the past. Concepts which are essentially atemporal, for example, 'the Anglo-Irish literary tradition', are confidently given dates. Take that specific example, confine it to women writers, and a kind of genealogy is forced to emerge: Maria Edgeworth, Mrs Oliphant (and other Irish-born genre writers of the late nineteenth century), Somerville and Ross, Lady Gregory, Christine Lady Longford, Elizabeth Bowen.

But does such a catalogue — even if it were in the most scholarly way amplified and rearranged — does it, can it, carry out the intentions of my title? They contain, after all, the same terms. But it cannot, firstly because the title is about women in a half-forgotten role — women as readers as well as writers — and the field is *relationships* between the four ideas 'Irish', 'women', 'modern' and 'writing'. To want to discuss relationships is to open up to speculation rather than to rest on conclusiveness.

And importantly, it is fraudulent to make pseudo-objective catalogues of writers and to leave the record at that. The catalogues themselves conceal a void. Consider: how impressive a catalogue can we make? Secondly, consider who or what constitutes the void that the catalogue, however extensive, does not cover? And then, what are the implications if, as I believe, the whole exercise raises questions that refer inward to incoherent experience rather than forward to the usual cohering aims of an essay?

The catalogue first. Decide to place the birth of modern Ireland at the death of Parnell. In Ireland, from that time to the present day, there has been no woman writer of the very highest ambition and achievement — no Emily Dickinson, no Dorothy Richardson, no Christina Stead. There have been, of course, a few women writers who are interesting, or honourable, or good. Mary Lavin, for one, and (in a derivative way) Elizabeth Bowen. *The Real Charlotte* is a graceful novel. Lucile Redmond writes real short stories. One, or perhaps two, excellent modern women poets have written, mainly in Irish. Well, one, Máire Mhac an tSaoi. Think harder: Kate O'Brien? Eavan Boland? Val Mulkerns? Julia O'Faolain? No. Argument there is about respecting and liking, but no one supposes that the argument is about a place in the pantheon, an election to a great tradition which itself does not exist. There are no woman playwrights whose plays would bear discussion. There is not, in the century or so I'm thinking about, an occasional, startling, womanly statement — no *Story of an African Farm*, no *Tell Me a Riddle*, no *Ethan Frome*. Only one Irish woman writer, Edna O'Brien, has reached a mass audience at home and abroad. There is no feminist Irish writer using the imaginative modes, or rather none with the philosophic range that would make her indispensable. I can imagine arguments for, say, Emma Cooke, or Mary Beckett, or Eithne Strong, or Leland Bardwell. But, if measured against the highest and the richest you could have, is there a single Irish woman writer in the English language whose work you would choose to preserve, let all the rest perish? Can the catalogue be revised to prove that there is?

And during that same century since Parnell, millions of Irish women lived. Their absence is the void. The period was that of nation-making and national consolidation, and in the imaginative arts of that time — in the artefacts, like novels, plays and poems, that are the only sure guide to why things happened as they did — there is a huge silence. That of women.

We begin to move towards the incoherent. Does it matter, and if so to whom and why, that our women's literature is so small and so thin? Does any significance attach, for the Irish woman, to this absence of any account of her own condition, an account which would have the basic authenticity of coming from another woman? Is the story of women and writing in Ireland merely the story of a passive audience? Has our view of ourselves been largely mediated by men, especially by Irish men?

If it does matter, where does it matter? To aspirant Irish women writers? To Irish women as a whole? Or only to a small number of Irish women who feel that to leave this kind of area unexplored is to help to lock Irish feminism into neo-male activism: to deprive it of a possible history, to impoverish its imagination, to accept a feminism which hasn't tried to make its own alphabet. Other women have taken literature and literary criticism and have used them to illuminate the present condition of the female. Mary Ellmann did it in *Talking About Women*. Kate Millett did it in *Sexual Politics*. The procedures of this kind of musing are unsound by the standards of academic criticism. But, however dubious the methodology, however bizarre the conclusions, there is a need to reclaim such unexamined territories of our intellectual world.

Why have so few Irish women been writers at all? Well, there are obvious reasons why there have always been fewer female than male writers — the reasons that have to do with class structure and literacy, the economic reasons which have, in modern times, driven the woman writer towards popular genres — ghost stories, romances, historical novelettes, pornography. It is easy to show how financial and biological freedom — and the presence of a male wife — have been the precondition for the best women's literary work (except for lyric poetry, which lives within the writer in herself and not the writer-in-her-world).

But there has been no condition applicable to Ireland from which women writers have not been able to escape. We are provincials. So was Katherine Mansfield. Ah, but we are disaffected provincials. Well, so is the Canadian Margaret Atwood. So is the American radical Marge Piercy, yet both have written good feminist novels. We are caught between ideologies — well so, in their way, were Lady Gregory during the first World War and Doris Lessing during the second: yet, of the two, which, from the conflict, made material that matters? In the English-speaking world, no woman in any country has an absolute defence, in socio-political terms, for silence. Even in police states, even outside literacy, women have made imaginative statements of great power. Neo-colonialism cannot, in this, be our defence.

Is our silence, then, the result of commonplace oppression by men — in the case of Irish women and writing, by men of genius? Modern Irish literature is dominated by men so brilliant in their misanthropy — the great and elegant series of chauvinists from Shaw and Wilde to Yeats, Joyce and Beckett — that if literature is a meaningful force, if it does arise from and reflect back upon the culture of its maker, if one knows that its truth is valid on a timescale far beyond the individual life, then the self-respect of Irish women is radically and paradoxically checkmated by respect for an Irish national achievement. These men transcended the literal. No woman did. And, having transcended the literal, they, *inter alia*, and as a consequence of modernism, denied the literal they knew, in the line of mothers, manageresses, wives, lovers and daughters, and imagined instead the figure-woman with whose stereotypes we now live

— the goddess, the slut and the hag. The counter-myth to these is the minor one of the saintly Irish mother. Joyce *had* such a mother but he needed more to reject than to know her and thus make us know her. Perhaps it is as well for Irish women that Joyce did not care to make women real. Were it possible to see Joyce enrolled as an ally of de Valera's vision of 'comely maidens' the two imaginations would establish a hegemony over the idealism of girls. There is a Stalinism of preferred behaviour which we would not have been able to resist, had Irish literature and Irish social politics been at one. But they were not. Schizophrenia is latent in the fact that the images of women in our greatest literature are urban, urbane and powerful. We are, in a social version, rural, innocent and the loving servants of males.

This is where the topic of women and Irish literature usually starts from. One can easily follow the Irish heroine — that impossible sister — through Pearse and Synge and into the doggerel of *Ireland's Own* emigrant poetry or the more interesting doggerel of Irish Country and Western lyrics. In this tradition, women are mindless and ferocious. One can easily learn, from Shaw to Beckett, also a tradition, that women are ferociously mindless. But to leave it at that, to assert that more and better literary ammunition fell on the heads of Irish women than on the heads of any comparable emergent modern group, and damaged the whole sex, would be almost to assert that we define ourselves by literature alone, that books kept us back. It's almost true. Those writers were, after all, Irish. Irish statesmen and ecclesiastics have, after all, oppressed us uniquely. The official version of great art was indeed, at least in the cases of Joyce and Yeats, great art. There has been a uniquely confusing array of patriarchal orders to obey. School and university had no alternative Irishness to offer, except the storehold locked behind the Irish language. Until the mid-fifties the only sexy Irish heroine was Molly Bloom, against whose image it might be said that the notion of sexiness and the concept of heroine are neither of them perceived by women or accepted by women in any negotiable way.

We inherit a country, modern Ireland, where the single imaginative construct we might admire — what Irish men did with words — is utterly at variance, in respect of images of women, with what the men who have power over us want us to be. In France, there's no particular reason why the woman who wants to live like Colette or her women should not do so. Our exemplars are socially impossible.

But the relation of women to women in books is not as simple as that. True, modern Irish literature — the work of men — is exceptional in its daring, its accomplishment and its influence. And its influence on women writers is even more inhibiting than its influence on all women as they think of themselves.

But the important point is that none of the great Irish writers are realists. It is not the intractability of Captain Barbara, or Gwendolyn, or Molly Bloom, or Maud Gonne, or Nell as exemplars which is the stumbling block — we do not live by exemplars or write by them in any obvious way — it is the absence of realism from our great literary tradition which obliterates women. Because realism is the only mode available to women writers who want to write to and of women, I do not mean that women could not and do not avail themselves of non-realist devices, but I do mean that the core of women's writing has always been confessional and has, in the last few decades, become autobiographical. Its ultimate realisation would be a realism based on personal realisation: but the ultimate in this or any other form of expression is only a guide here.

At the same time as women are conscious of themselves as representative, every woman's condition is profoundly a shared one. The ideal feminist novel would be known by other women to tell the truth, the truth about the individual and about the condition. It would demand a super-realism. And that brief, if it were accepted, would go back to strike at the roots of the novel itself, as well it might if the novel is the literary form most responsive to bourgeois individualism, and if individualism is itself a construct of capitalist males. A womanly novel has to be, and yet theoretically cannot be, a realist novel. And yet the novel is the necessary form of communication between sister and sister. Just as we need a minimum of mutually understood language to communicate, just as adult humans need to see in another an adult human before speaking, so novels contain an irreducible element of the real world, and that element is the medium of trust between writer and reader. The real world is not just a matter of tables and chairs, but of money and time and universal hopes, disappointments and accommodations. And that whole area of realism, above the shared material facts of furniture — the area where the structures of life, economic, political, are determinants of human potential — is the area which conscious women believe is tainted. The structures were made by the power-holders. Women do not know how deeply they are implicated, how un-female they have been, in consenting at all to the world as it is. We know no other world than this we are in, but we deeply suspect it. Yet we cannot share this or any world without that description of this world which is the basis of the novel as a social agent.

There is no other social agent of comparable scope. The lyric poem floats free of condition. Sociology offends the strength of individual experience. Listening to women talk — in person, in journalism, on radio and television — reflects back upon the listening self which will pick and choose from actuality, shapelessly. The novel compresses events and options, makes decisions about description in every line, chooses the space between beginning and ending.

Novels seem to be like life, though they are not, and it is the seeming, while not being, that makes them both persuasive and unthreatening. The women's movement may have begun with non-fiction books like *The Feminine Mystique, The Female Eunuch, The Second Sex*, but its mass audience was won by the novels of Erica Jong, Marilyn French, Marge Piercy, Mary Gordon, Margaret Atwood. These books constitute a literature. It makes no difference to their importance, when there is this quantity of women's books within a culture, that some or even all of them are formally naive or philosophically questionable. It is as a body that North America can be said to have a women's literature.

To return to the Irish situation — these same books matter to us although they are all, by definition, alien. Their overall importance is misunderstood because comprehensive distribution is given only to the sensational and overtly sexual writers. The mechanics of distribution are the fascist government of what we think of as a democracy of reading and writing. What happens from the publisher's acceptance of an author to the point where a book comes into the hands of a reader has so little to do with individual expression that it distorts all arguments about culture. Yet commerce is a reflection of culture too, and Edna O'Brien is arguably the most important writer in modern Ireland by sole virtue of the fact that her books can be found on the revolving book-stand of any small-town Irish newsagent's shop. She is published, advertised and distributed. Not one other native woman writer is, in those respects, comparable.

Of course she is a good writer as well, a serious and formally ambitious one, even, in a novel like *Night* or a story like 'The Love Object' an impressive one. But she was perhaps limited by her time.

Edna O'Brien was an expression of the post-de Valera, contemporary Ireland when she began to write. Whether she was at the time of her first few books a 'woman's' as distinct from a woman writer, is open to question. Certainly she is not a feminist since she is unwilling to analyse, but rather evokes her heroines' romantic masochism. She is indifferent to non-romantic situations of any dramatic power. Her recurring vivid moment is the moment of loss: loss of a man. There is much more to be learned about loss from Leopold Bloom. But how many Irish women readers know and care nothing about Bloom, while striving to read every word of Edna O'Brien's, because she is a woman, a modern woman, one of us?

One comes at last to the simple difficulty at the heart of the title, 'Irish Women and Writing in Modern Ireland'. All four elements in the phrase belong to different chronologies. Women as an 'us' (I date that from Simone de Beauvoir and Betty Friedan) have only about twenty-five years of history. Modern Ireland is about, say, sixty years old. And literature, at least in the form of the novel, is aged, perhaps, four hundred. Juggling with the terms is like juggling with plates of different size and weight, which I presume to be, if not impossible, then an exercise in pointless virtuosity. The element which I am supposed to be considering is the history of literature, itself as old, obviously, as the subject itself, but as an academic construct about a century old. But as a woman who watches what books other women avidly borrow and talk about and weigh against their own lives, I know that the largely American novels of the last twenty years are the element that my community cares about. History is almost contemporaneous. Then the adjective Irish. On one hand, within the history of literature, being Irish is to have a large, if vicarious, share in great triumphs. On the other hand, to women newly conscious of themselves, being Irish is neither here nor there, except to know that a vicarious share in male triumphs is no share at all. Inside feminism there is a desire to wipe history out: it was not ours, but the future might be. But inside feminists there are women, and women have always been forced to be reasonable and to compromise with the given facts. What is the relationship between conscious women and any history?

I have proposed that there has not been a great Irish woman writer. The minor women writers have had inconsiderable audiences. That non-Irish women writers speak from social worlds we do not know. And that novelists, not broadcasters or politicians or the woman next door, are our mentors. These propositions isolated Edna O'Brien, but that in itself raised a further questio . Her first book was published more than twenty years ago. A revolution in women's self-consciousness has happened since. Does nobody else have anything to say? Or is the need for self-expression perfectly met by the foreign, especially American, novels of the last few decades? As if women are more similar in their dreams and their despair than they are different in their cultures and societies? If it is so, then the topic 'Irish Women and Writing in Modern Ireland' is already outmoded. It was never of great importance. It is essentially finished if there is now a literature to satisfy the woman reader which has nothing to do with Irishness. By extension, there is no pressure on an Irish woman writer of today to write at all — her social and cultural uniqueness is only of interest, not of value, in an international world. So that the final element in precluding an Irish women's literature in the solidarity of women itself.

But of course there is something wrong with an argument that supposes that literature, which is made of individual attempts at perfection of expression, could be annihilated by mere writing which is, after all, what most feminist novels are. They are, on the whole, very bad. There are many reasons why they are so bad. The classic English novel is itself an artefact of bourgeois individualism and therefore a male-structured artefact, however many women have used it as writer or reader. An intelligent feminist like Marilyn French treats its conventions with deliberate carelessness; Monique Wittig subverts them. Secondly, the women's movement is not so much collectively self-indulgent as specific-ally opposed to critical hierarchies, as to all hierarchies, and this ideal has subverted the normal processes of discrimination. Thirdly, the real hunger of women readers for confessional women writers has made quality unimportant.

It is on the nature of this hunger that the argument for the future of women's literature turns. There have been other movements in the history of the novel — the 'Gothic', for example, mother of all horror fiction, or the 'silver fork', mother of *Princess Daisy*. These two 'schools' answered immediate needs, as feminist novels do now, and each dominated recorded literary fashion for only a short time — one might say the last three decades of the eighteenth century for the former and 1860—90 for the latter. Yet the needs these kinds of novel met were permanent. The sexuality of the Gothic novel and the social escapism of the 'silver fork' school are ineradicably attractive in the world as we know it. So that although these kinds of novel are said by historians to have become archaic, they have in fact simply moved down and broadened out into the simplest form of literature, the novelette, and nothing has dislodged them from the mass affection of the mass literate audience.

It is conceivable that women's movement literature will also join that underground and express such themes as mother-daughter relationships, the theme of bisexuality, the theme of households that are not families, the theme of fearless liberation of a woman's sexual, intellectual and social power. But those are the relatively glamorous themes. The more complex themes — total mistrust of men allied to need for men; fear of male institutions yoked to an incapacity to imagine non-male alternatives; love of children allied to a hatred of maternality, and especially the desire for pure freedom allied to the certain knowledge of being economically, biologically and politically unfree — those are not themes simple enough to enter popular reading. Not because the mass audience is stupid, but because life is hard. In so far as we know about mass popular literature we know that the conditions of the reader's life preclude effort. But if we do not grapple with these subjects as themes, we can and do accept them transposed to attitudes, as in the many popular novelettes where women disco-owners, restaurateurs, fashion experts, PR people, are the heroes/heroines of the tale by having money, sexuality and energy to a degree that the men have not. A bland progressiveness is now an assumption of the American novelette. But that is not enough for Ireland.

It follows that the responsibility for restating a woman's position will continue to fall back upon individual woman writers, and it follows again that a culture with no woman writers as such will remain unexpressed. There is no ground for shame in the fact that there never was an Irish woman writer to bear comparison with Joyce or Yeats or Beckett. What would matter would be to tacitly find such a creature unimaginable. Because Edna O'Brien existed, we are able to imagine a certain kind of Irish girl and Irish woman, one of exceptional and vigorous melancholy, one of terrible dependence on love, but a woman, nevertheless, from a recognisable landscape. There are other landscapes to be described, and there is not, as far as I know, a woman writer in Ireland today who is willing to describe them for us, to accomplish a description of us. Not yet.

Perhaps we lack such a writer as a consequence of our general lack of human rights. No Irish woman has ever been a great industrialist, or jurist or labour leader. Or writer. It's as if the literary accomplishment falls among the other prohibited accomplishments. Practically speaking it should not. But who can say where exactly the *Zeitgeist* has its home? Is it not plausible to suggest that women who are grossly unfree should obscure their private centre, from which only a novel might be written? Erica Jong earned millions of dollars and love and admiration for her two books. My point is not that her odyssey in search of self-love would be unrewarded in this country: it is that no Irish woman, furtive as we are to the nerve, would expose herself as she did. We may love ourselves as much as she does herself, but no-one is ever going to know. And if we won't tell anyone about ourselves — because the penalty is still obloquy and exile — then how can anyone hear us? Admittedly, to rely on a theory of the Irish female psyche is a weak way to leave an argument. But it is where I choose to leave it, knowing well that an argument from historical circumstance, from the history of education, from sociology, from, even, a theory of chance, would be more convincing. I choose to rest, not exactly on intuition, but on an unverifiable personal belief. There is no summing up in the asking of a question.

And this brings me back to my beginning, where I wondered what modern Ireland is, and where, in our imagination of time, we have placed its birth. We do not know. We ourselves enter the subject of Irish women and writing at the moment in our own lives when we became conscious of ourselves, our female selves, our person among the people of the nation, our inner selves alert to the ebb and flow of books. Modern Ireland begins for us when we make our first political act: what the historians offer as modern Ireland is an abstraction which becomes real to us only when we act in relation to it. And if this is a ruthlessly subjective way of coming to the notion of 'Irish women' it is nothing to be ashamed of. Go even further. Reading and writing and what it does to one is an even more personal matter. Irish women and writing begins and ends in thousands upon thousands of singular experiences. And if the perfect and confirming experience has not yet happened here, and even if it never does, what matters is to value the woman writer, the mode of literature and the woman reader in such a way that the idea of their coming together is a specific hope in a general optimism.

Notes on the Authors

MARY COLEMAN is Society Secretary for Country Markets in Ireland. She has lectured in Ireland and the United States on lacemaking. In 1977 she founded the Guild of Irish Lacemakers.

MIRIAM DALY See page XXX

HELEN LANIGAN WOOD is curator of the Fermanagh County Museum and a member of the Historic Movements Advisory Council. Formerly a field archaeologist with the Archaeological Survey. Belfast and the National Monuments Branch Dublin, her *Images of Stone* (Blackstaff), a study of figure sculpture in the Lough Erne Basin was published in 1976.

DR PATRICIA LYSAGHT is a lecturer in the Department of Irish Folklore at University College Dublin. She has previously published articles on the subject of the Banshee.

PAULA McCARTHY-PANCZENKO is President of the Ireland America Arts Exchange, Mass. USA. She has previously held posts in the Arts Council of Ireland and in the Wexford Arts Centre. Her essay 'Great Expectations: Ireland's Hopes and Heritage come together in the Arts', was published in the *American Arts Magazine* 1982. She is a member of the International Art Cities Association and of the Art Historians Association.

DR MARGARET MacCURTAIN is a lecturer in the Department of History at University College Dublin. She is co-editor of *Women in Irish Society* (Arlen House).

EILÉAN NÍ CHUILLEANÁIN is a senior lecturer in English at Trinity College Dublin. She has published articles on Renaissance and modern literature, as well as four collections of poems, the most recent being *The Rose-Geranium* (1981). She is co-editor of *Cyphers*, a literary magazine.

NOIRÍN NÍ RIAIN is a professional singer, who has studied music at University College, Cork. She received the MA degree (on the subject of 'Traditional Religious Songs in Irish') in 1980. Her two recordings of Traditional Religious Songs with the Monks of Glenstal Abbey have been widely acclaimed.

NUALA O'FAOLAIN is a television producer with Radio Telefis Éireann and has also worked as producer with the British Broadcasting Corporation. She has also lectured in English at University College Dublin and NIHE.

YVONNE SCANNELL is a lecturer in Law at Trinity College Dublin. She is a member of the European Council for Environmental Law and of the International Council for Environmental Law. Work previously published includes *The Law and Practice Relating to Pollution Control in Ireland* (1976, 2nd ed. 1982) and several articles on environmental law and women's rights. She is Vice Chairperson of the Women's Political Association.

Index.